Grace

In

Texas

Danette Fogarty

To our daughter,

Elizabeth Grace

Find all the love

you can!

Love, Mommy

Dear Readers,

I love the way Grace and Tavin meet and how they must overcome some pretty big emotional obstacles. Much like real life, things are complicated. I hope you enjoy the characters and enjoy seeing what Raelynn and Seth are up to.

A Love as Big as Texas Series:

Book 1: Jumping Back Into Love

Book 2: Grace in Texas

Book 3: Lawyer Up, Cowboy

Please enjoy the scenery as much as the characters. I wrote these books to encompass Brazoria County, Texas where we live. Things really are bigger in Texas.

Thank you,

Danette

Chapter 1

The phone was ringing so Grace rolled over in her bed and grabbed for it on the nightstand.

"Hello," She mumbled groggily.

Laughter came through the phone, "Grace?" Melissa asked.

Sitting up, Grace rubbed her eyes, "Yes, this is Grace," she said hesitantly.

Melissa found it funny that her niece didn't know who was calling. If it weren't so important, she would take pleasure in messing with Grace for a bit.

"Well, if you wouldn't sleep in, you'd be awake enough to know this is your Aunt Melissa." Melissa couldn't help but be a little sarcastic.

Shaking her head, and smiling, Grace sat up. "Funny," She answered dryly.

After looking at the clock and seeing it was barely eight in the morning, Grace wondered if something was wrong.

"Are you okay?" Grace asked her aunt.

Always the sweet child, Melissa thought to herself. "Yes, thank you." Melissa sighed, "Actually I have a job proposition for you."

The statement made Grace sit up straighter and wake up fully. A job proposition?

Grace dutifully reached for her pad of paper and pen off of her nightstand, "I'm listening," she started.

Just hearing her niece's voice made Melissa feel overcome with emotion. She and Grace were two peas in a pod; everyone said so. Ever since she first laid eyes on her niece, she was the child Melissa never got around to having. They were inseparable over the summers Grace spent visiting in Texas. That was until the summer after her senior year.

Something happened but Grace never said what it was, she just stopped coming for visits. Now, with things so crazy, Melissa thought maybe now was the time for them to get past it.

"Well," Melissa said, "it seems as though Raelynn is now with child and her bratty OB/GYN has insisted she spend the rest of her pregnancy in bed."

Hearing the dramatic tone in her aunt's voice, Grace couldn't help but smile. Melissa was the kindest person she knew and she would NEVER think such a thing about her best friend. She just put up the best pretenses about serious things. Grace appreciated that trait.

Clearing her throat, Grace smirked, "How rude of him!"

"I know right," Melissa answered smartly. "Anyway, I know you're in the middle of an intern thing but I was hoping you might be able to come down and help out."

Surprised by the offer, Grace wasn't sure how to answer. Aunt Melissa and her friend, Raelynn Rhodes, ran a CPA firm and Grace was in the middle of an internship to earn credits for her Environmental Studies degree. The two things didn't seem to jive.

Thinking about it, Grace knew Aunt Melissa wouldn't call her unless it was important. Family was important.

"Tell me what you need," Grace answered.

Melissa sighed. "I need someone I can trust to come in and help out with our clients, running the office and our interns, and basically keeping me from going bonkers."

Grace chuckled and asked. "Okay, what's in it for me?"

'Oh yes, two peas in a pod,' Melissa said to herself. "I've got free room and board and twenty dollars an hour."

Eyebrows raised, Grace quickly did the math. She could work for Aunt Melissa and make a pretty good amount of money in a few months.

Nodding, Grace contemplated what she could do. Her internship was up next week, no doubt what prompted her aunt to make the offer. She was taking a semester off anyway to save up money for her senior year and this could really help.

"Okay," Grace said, "you've got a deal."

Melissa laughed, "Whoo hoo!"

They spoke for an hour about what would be involved, when Grace could start, and how she would get down to Texas.

After hanging up with her aunt, Grace texted her brother Brad to let him in on her plans.

This was certainly an about face to her plans but Grace felt like it was right.

Grace was getting dressed when she got the response from her brother. She laughed at the expletives he used. It was crazy, even she could see that. But if it helped her aunt and herself, why should she pass it by?

It wouldn't be easy to convince Brad, or her parents for that matter, but they would just need to deal with her decisions. After all, they all wanted her to be a "grown up" and get herself through school.

For three years Grace worked her tail off to pay for her college education. Her parents could afford it but they thought having their children pay for their own education was a better learning experience.

Grace and Brad spent a lot of nights wondering why they had to do this but, in the end, they figured their parents couldn't say anything about how they got their education if they didn't pay for it.

Figuring she spent enough time being lazy, Grace got up and started to clean and plan out her weekend. She would need to give notice at her apartment complex and get boxes to pack up her belongings. The furnishings were included so she only needed to move her personal stuff.

Brad texted her on and off during the day and helped her plan out her trip.

By the next morning, Grace felt confident with her decisions.

Two weeks later, she was putting the last of her boxes in a small moving trailer hooked up to Brad's SUV. He was kind enough to store her stuff while she was in Texas.

"How're you doing?" Brad asked as Grace closed the trailer.

Grace turned to her brother and smiled, "Kind of excited actually," she answered.

Nodding, Brad grabbed her for a quick hug, "Just be safe okay."

Not wanting to cry, Grace just nodded back. She would miss her brother. They lived only a half hour from one another, choosing colleges nearby. This would be the first time in three years he wasn't close enough to lean on. Of course, Aunt Melissa would be there but still.

Grace hugged her brother one last time and walked to her car. Brad stood by her door until she was buckled in.

Pulling away, Grace watched her brother wave in her rearview mirror and tried not to cry.

It was early November in Virginia so the air was cold. The leaves were falling into piles of red, orange, and gold along the tree lines. Grace knew she would miss that part of living here, the definitive change in seasons.

The Texas temperatures were still in the high 70's and Aunt Melissa told her to only bring a few light layers.

The trip down south took Grace from Virginia down through North Carolina. After she passed the Raleigh area, it was all smaller towns and rolling hills.

Grace decided to stop just shy of the South Carolina border to have a light lunch.

She pulled into a diner right off the 95 Freeway and smiled at the brightly painted sign that said "MO'S."

When she walked inside, Grace smiled brighter. The walls were a bright green and dotted with pictures of, what she assumed were, locals.

After she was seated in a booth done up in a cream colored upholstery, a slender, but smiling woman came up to her table. Grace studied the woman's hair done in a beehive hairdo and noticed that she was chomping gum.

"Hello there, sweetie," The woman said in a southern twang, "what can I get ya?"

Grace smiled, "Well,.......Melinda," she repeated the name on the woman's nametag, "I think I'll have a diet soda and take a minute to decide. Can you recommend anything?"

Chomp, snap, chomp, Melinda smiled sweetly, "Sweetie, everything is good," she leaned in, "but I'd go for the hot turkey sandwich, it's Bob's specialty."

Nodding, Grace leaned in toward Melinda, "I think I'll have that then," she replied and winked at the spunky waitress.

"You got it," Melinda said and walked away.

'What a character,' Grace thought.

After a nice lunch, Grace walked around the adjoining convenience store next to MO's and got a few snacks. Once she was back on the road, she put in a CD of her favorite music and let her mind drift as she made her way south.

She thought about Aunt Melissa and realized how much she missed her aunt the last couple of years.

When she was younger, going to Texas was the highlight of her year.

Her parents were great people but steeped deeply in academia. Grace and her brother were very good students but it was so nice to have the time away from that intensity, even if it was only for about eight weeks in the summer.

Aunt Melissa took her to the roller skating rink, or swimming, or horseback riding. It was always an adventure and Grace loved it.

During her last summer visit, she had no idea it was going to end so badly.

'Stop!' Grace demanded of herself. There was no use going down that road. It only led to a bunch of 'what ifs' and it was too late for that.

She was an adult now and wasn't going to make a fool of herself.

Resigned to follow her own advice, Grace turned up the music and sang along to some party songs.

The next time she stopped, she was well into South Carolina. She navigated her way easily through Columbia, grateful she wasn't hitting traffic during rush hour. After dealing with the city congestion, she needed a quick break and decided to stop for gas.

It took a little bit to find a place right off of the freeway that looked friendly.

As she pulled up to the gas pump, Grace saw a man come out of the station. He was sixty if he was a day! And he wore a big smile as he walked over to the driver side of the vehicle.

"Afternoon," He greeted the pretty, young lady who pulled up.

Grace smiled, "Good afternoon." She was going to get out but he pulled the nozzle out and stood there waiting.

The man smiled, "What can I getcha?" He asked.

"Uh," Grace said, "how about 87."

She was very surprised by the man's behavior and got out.

Grace smiled, "I can get that," she said, not knowing what to do.

"Oh, it's part of the service," The man replied.

Peeking over, she saw that his nametag said, Gary. "Thank you, Gary," She said.

Smiling, the man shook his head, "I'm Pete." He nodded toward the building, "Gary's my brother."

As if on cue, a man poked his head out of the station and waved, "Howdy!" He yelled.

If the men weren't so nice, Grace was pretty sure she would have laughed.

Southern hospitality was in full swing and she was glad for it.

After he finished filling up her car, Pete took her credit card and walked inside with Grace following him.

The inside was clean and tidy and, obviously, very well taken care of.

It turned out that Pete and Gary were twins who ran the gas station their parents opened up 50 years earlier. They ran it the exact same way their dad did up until he died.

Grace pulled out of the station and waved to the brothers thinking how great it was to meet such genuinely nice people.

This trip was getting more interesting by the minute.

Three hours later, Grace was on the last bit of her trip for the day and navigating through the traffic around Atlanta, Georgia.

Unfortunately, it was now well into rush hour so the cars were going intermittently. The stress of being in an unknown area and trying to find her way through the city was wearing on Grace's nerves.

It took well over an hour to get around the city and she finally was able to breathe easier as she turned onto the 85 Freeway South.

The darkness swept in early so that, combined with being tired from the long drive, put Grace on edge again.

When her GPS told her to turn off for her hotel she smiled with relief.

The hotel was right off the freeway so that was good. It was a chain that was very reliable. Grace smiled remembering that Brad insisted she stay somewhere "safe."

After checking in, Grace went upstairs and into her room. It was clean and nice and a place to lay her head. The day was pleasant but she was beat after spending so many hours in the car.

Luckily, she grabbed some stuff to snack on from the stop in South Carolina so she pulled out the bag.

Once she was showered and changed, she sat on the bed. She got out the bags of snacks, a bottled water, and turned on the TV.

Having a full stomach and a place to rest, Grace fell asleep quickly with the words from the movie droning softly in the background.

Chapter 2

Grace was sitting on the roof of her car, looking out over the lake. A group of them were parked near the water's edge, the lights from the cars illuminating the area until they could get the bonfire going.

She was feeling a little bad that she told Hailey a lie about where she was going.

Raelynn's daughter was her friend but she was only fourteen and the group here were all seniors. Grace wanted to hang out, just this once, with kids her own age.

She was still sitting there watching the guys gather the firewood up into a pile when she heard a noise behind her.

It was dark so she couldn't see who was there.

"Hello?" She asked into the darkness.

There was no answer.

Curious, Grace hopped down onto the grass and started to make her way behind the car.

There was a line of trees maybe thirty feet from where the group parked. When her eyes were adjusted to the darkness, she could make out a shape.

"Hello," She said again, a little louder than before.

The shape emerged from behind some trees a little ways in front of her.

She could see that it was a man. He was tall and she could see the silhouette of him but not his features.

"You shouldn't be here," The deep voice of the shape replied.

Instead of being afraid, which Grace should have been, she was excited.

Just the sound of his voice made her skin tingle. She moved closer, trying to figure out if she knew him.

Grace stepped closer, "Do I know you?" she asked softly.

The shape moved out from the shadows of the trees and she could see some features of his face in the reflection of the light.

"Hello," Grace said and wondered why her heart was beating so fast.

The man stepped closer, "Hello," he said back.

He was tall, that was for sure. Grace saw that he stood almost a foot taller than she was. His shoulders were broad and he smelled heavenly. All male.

Trying to see him clearer, Grace moved to the side, "I'm Grace," she whispered.

She hoped he would answer with his name since he avoided the question she asked a few seconds earlier.

For some reason her voice escaped her so she just stood there staring at him.

"TJ," Was his response.

Grace's mouth formed an o. 'TJ,' she said in her mind. 'That's a cowboy name.'

Not sure what to do now, Grace just stood there and wondered if she should reach out to touch him. The decision was taken out of her hand when the figure named TJ took her hand into his.

Her mother, she was pretty sure, would be screaming at her to get away from this person since she didn't know who he was. For some reason though, Grace just stood there and let him hold her hand.

"I've noticed you," TJ said.

Blushing, Grace wasn't sure how to respond and just said, "Oh."

She was so stupid! Her chest was heaving and she wondered what would happen when she felt him shift and move even closer.

Before she could say anything else, TJ bent down and gently touched his lips to hers.

'His lips are so soft,' Grace thought. She wasn't very experienced with kissing but she certainly knew the basics. This guy was good!

She thought her heart would leap out of her chest when his tongue touched her lips, asking silently for entry.

Grace opened up for him and allowed him to explore. The feel of his tongue on hers was a game changer. What started out as a gentle exploration burst into a combustible wave of passion.

Closing her eyes, Grace tried to feel everything. She had to grab on to TJ's shoulders to keep from falling over. When his arms came around her and pulled her close, she felt the crush of her chest into his and moaned at the sensations it caused inside of her.

She felt lightheaded and free. Her hands roamed up and down his shoulders and dove into his hair. She thought it felt like silk against her fingertips.

His hand slip up under her t-shirt and brushed across her ribcage. The feeling caused Grace to jerk back quickly. Even though they were no longer touching, Grace's lips still tingled.

"I," She started, embarrassed that she was so shy.

TJ cleared his throat, "I apologize," he said quietly.

Grace was going to say no when she saw him turn and leave.

She just stood there and wondered if the whole thing really happened when she heard her friends calling her.

Two days later, Grace was with Hailey at the local hangout when she felt the hairs on her neck stand up.

When she turned around, she saw the most handsome man she'd ever seen standing there and staring at her.

Smiling, Grace motioned for Hailey to come with her as she started walking toward him.

She knew, instinctively, that this was the man who kissed her in the woods. And, he was even more handsome than she imagined.

He wore jeans, cowboy boots, a t-shirt, and a baseball cap and made the casual clothes look sexy.

Grace was about to say something when she heard Hailey beside her.

"TJ," Hailey said excitedly and ran a few feet to hug him.

Not knowing what to say, Grace just stood there. It was him! She was sure of it now. Hailey knew him? Even better because now it would be okay for Grace to be around him.

TJ smiled and hugged Hailey quickly, "Squirt," he said and tapped her nose with his finger. "What are you doing here?"

Hailey smiled at his attention, "Oh this is my friend Grace. She's a senior."

Grace couldn't mistake the look of shock that ran across TJ's face when he heard what Hailey said. Confused, she stepped forward, sure that he would acknowledge her.

"Hi," Grace said softly.

TJ nodded to her, "Hi," he responded.

Before Grace could say anything, TJ reached into his pocket and handed Hailey some money.

"Squirt," He said to Hailey, "can you get me a soda? I'll keep Grace company."

Nodding, Hailey smiled and said, "Okay."

Once Hailey left to go toward the counter to get the soda, TJ turned to face Grace.

"How old are you?" He demanded in a tight whisper.

What did her age have to do with it? Grace was confused and asked, "Why do you want to know?"

She watched as TJ's face paled. "You're not an adult are you," He muttered through clenched teeth. "Sweet Jesus!"

Again, confused, Grace didn't know what the problem was. "I was wondering where you went to the other night," She looked around to make sure Hailey was still getting his soda, "I felt bad about not talking to you."

Grace waited for him to say something, anything, but he stood there looking really mad.

Hailey came back just then and handed him his soda.

"Well, it was nice to meet you Grace," TJ said coolly then winked at Hailey before turning to go.

Wanting to cry, Grace didn't know what to do about TJ's odd reaction. She looked from Hailey to his retreating form and back again.

Finally, Grace turned to Hailey, "Can you wait here for a second? I want to ask TJ something." She smiled at a nodding Hailey and ran after TJ.

Grace caught up to him as he was getting into his truck. "Hey," She said in a breathy voice, "what's wrong?"

In her opinion, they shared an awesome kiss. She didn't think he was against it if her body was any indication. She felt his response to her and that was not something she made up.

"What's wrong?" TJ shot back, "You're just a kid!"

The words hurt….. a lot! "I'm not," She countered.

TJ was about to put the truck in drive but stopped and turned to look at her.

Grace saw the look of disgust on his face and it made her want to cower down. She held her ground though, and stared at him.

Shaking his head, TJ growled, "I don't have time for some kid."

He put the truck into gear and peeled out, leaving Grace standing there, rejected.

Grace woke up in a sweat. Holy Cow! She hadn't dreamed about TJ in a very long time.

Getting up, she took a few deep breaths. The feeling of hurt and rejection were still strong. She left Texas, and her aunt, two weeks after the infamous TJ broke her heart and hadn't been back since.

'How could a man do that?' She asked herself for the gazillionth time.

'Well, he probably doesn't even live there anymore,' she thought to herself as she went into the bathroom.

After she came out she looked at her phone and saw she had about an hour before she had to get up and get moving for the day.

She laid back down and tried to fall back asleep but, instead, kept thinking about the handsome man who said the most hurtful things to her.

Laying there, she was embarrassed to admit that he was the reason she didn't go back to Texas to visit her aunt. She was afraid of running into him again and feeling all the crazy, wonderful things he made her feel but hearing all the awful things he said.

Four years later, the pain was still raw.

"You're an adult now," Grace said out loud.

Getting up, she started to get her things together. She was an adult and, as such, needed to get a grip.

She turned on the TV and listened to the news and weather as she got ready.

It was a little after nine when she made her way downstairs for the continental breakfast the hotel put out.

Settling on a piece of toast and some juice, Grace sat down next to an older couple and ate her breakfast quietly.

When it was time to go, she checked out and put her overnight bag in the trunk of her car.

Before long, she was back on the highway and heading south through Georgia.

The day went by fast, Grace electing to stop twice for some food and gas.

She left Georgia and drove through Alabama and into Mississippi. The lushness of the greenery, along with the milder temperatures, made the drive nice.

She was on the 10 Freeway and knew this was the last stretch.

As she crossed into Louisiana, Grace was relieved she was almost there.

The dream that plagued her the night before cost her some much needed sleep and that made driving even more difficult.

She wasn't in a bad mood, just a little on edge. She spent the majority of the ride wondering if she would see the notorious TJ again and, more importantly, what she would say to him if she did.

Rehearsing snappy comebacks made the time pass quickly. She imagined that he came crawling up to her, begging her to kiss him once again and she was able to reject him as he did to her.

It wasn't like Grace to be rude or vindictive.

She stopped in Lake Charles, Louisiana one last time before pushing on into Texas.

It was late afternoon so the traffic was easy. After she pulled into a truck stop, she got out and stretched.

Her shoulders were tight from stress and she grimaced as she rotated them in an effort to loosen up.

Grace walked inside and smiled at the people she passed on her way to the restroom.

Even if she was upset, she made an effort to be polite and kind to others. It wasn't their fault that a jackass broke her heart a few years ago.

Shaking her head at her own thoughts, Grace walked out and grabbed a bottled water.

She took it up to the counter and got ready to pay.

"Hello there, beautiful," The male cashier said with a smile.

Grace couldn't help but return it. The compliment helped soothe her wounded ego.

He rung up her water and winked as she handed him the money.

"Bye," She said as she grabbed her water and walked out.

Apparently not every guy thought she wasn't worth it!

Less than an hour later, Grace smiled when she saw the 'Welcome to Texas' sign. Almost there.

She called her aunt on her Bluetooth and waited.

"Hello," Melissa answered the phone on the second ring.

Grace smiled, "Auntie, I'm in Texas," she said smugly.

Melissa let out a whoop, "Great!"

"I should be there in about two and half hours or so okay?" Grace asked.

Closing the folder she was working on, Melissa sighed, "Yes, that's perfect, I'll be at home waiting."

Grace hung up and kept smiling.

Aunt Melissa lived in a cute little house about five minutes from where she worked. It was nice and homey and Grace always felt welcomed when she would come to visit.

As she pulled into the driveway, she felt the warm memory embrace her. Aunt Melissa was standing on the front porch waving.

"You're here!" Melissa shouted as she crossed the yard to where her niece was getting out of her car.

Grace grinned wide, "I'm here!" She yelled back.

Melissa gathered her niece into her arms and held her tight. Oh how she missed Grace. Their time together before was so special to Melissa and she was glad they would have some time together now.

Chapter 3

After her aunt released her, Grace stepped back to get a good look at her. She was gorgeous in Grace's eyes. Her aunt was the woman Grace wanted to be when she was growing up.

"You look fantastic!" Grace said enthusiastically.

Melissa blushed, "Thank you sweetie, you are still gorgeous." She returned.

They walked into the house.

As soon as Grace was in her aunt's house, she felt like she was home. The furniture was different, probably updated since she was here last, but the same pictures were on the walls and it still smelled like fresh flowers.

Going into the kitchen, Melissa pulled out a pitcher of tea and poured two glasses.

"I can't believe you're here," She said with emotion to her niece.

Smiling, Grace took the glass and said, "I know."

They sat down at the dining room table.

Grace looked out the sliding door that led to the backyard. There was still a rocker glider out on the patio, flower beds around the edges, and a giant tree farther back. It was difficult not to reminisce about all the fun she had here while growing up.

Melissa watched her niece and knew she was thinking about her visits here when she was younger. It was a shame she hadn't been back in so long but, she was here now, and that was all that mattered.

"Okay," Melissa said as she put her glass of tea down. "Let's get you settled in and decide what you'd like for dinner."

Nodding, Grace was going to answer her when the phone rang. Her aunt hopped up and grabbed for it quickly, a big smile planted on her face.

Melissa leaned against the wall in the kitchen, "Hello there," she said in a sultry whisper.

'Well, well,' Grace thought. Hmmmm, it seems her aunt had a special someone now.

Wanting to give Melissa some privacy, Grace got up and walked out to her car to grab her bags.

She was still pulling bags from the trunk a few minutes later when Melissa came out of the house.

"I'm sorry about that, sweetie," Melissa said as she grabbed a bag to take inside.

Grace shook her head, "Don't be," she smiled as they started walking back inside. "I just better get some details."

Melissa blushed, "We're just dating," she explained as they took the bags upstairs to the guest room Grace would be using.

Grace pursed her lips, not sure if she should believe the word "just" her aunt used. If her look was any indication, this wasn't a "just dating" thing at all.

They placed the bags on the floor in front of the closet door and went back down for the rest.

"Okay," Grace said, "but still, details."

Laughing, Melissa nodded, "Okay," she answered.

The two of them got the rest of Grace's bags upstairs and Melissa left her alone to get settled.

Grace couldn't stop smiling.

Maybe it was because she was here with her aunt or maybe it was because she could see love in her aunt's eyes.

Melissa was always the rebel of their family, at least that's what Grace's mother always said. She never got married and moved down to Texas after college.

Personally, Grace thought that having that kind of independence was the best part of her aunt's life.

She put away her clothes, thankful that the closet was big enough for all of her things, and went back downstairs.

Coming down the hallway, Grace could hear voices.

When she entered the kitchen, Grace stopped in the doorway.

Her aunt was sitting at the dining table, her hands wrapped up in those of a very big cowboy.

They hadn't noticed her so she stood there and looked at them.

She suspected that this was the guy her aunt was talking to on the phone earlier and could see why her aunt blushed.

He was big, towering over her aunt's petite form. Even sitting down, Grace guessed he must stand well over six feet. His face was tanned and he looked…….tough.

Grace was still standing there when his eyes met hers and she blushed for getting caught staring.

He cleared his throat and stood up. Grace looked up and wanted to laugh because he was so big.

"Hi," Grace said and stuck out her hand to shake his.

She looked down as her hand was engulfed into his. He shook his firmly, but not like he was trying to break her hand or anything.

"Hello," He said a little hesitantly.

Melissa stood up and turned around, "Grace this is John," she said.

'Ahhh,' Grace thought to herself. Yep, her aunt was crazy, ga-ga over this guy.

Grace looked back at him, "Hi John," she said and felt silly since she just said hi to him.

Feeling a little easier, John released her hand and put his hands in his pockets. He was nervous to meet Melissa's niece.

"Your aunt says you're going to be helping her with the business while Raelynn's on bed rest," John said.

Liking the sound of his voice, Grace cocked her head slightly, "Yes, that's what I'm supposed to do."

There was a question there. "But what are you going to do?" John asked and winked.

Getting his teasing, Grace thought she would really like John. He kind of looked a little like a bull in a china shop in the midst of her aunt's kitchen but he was sincere and would be fun to hang around with.

Grace looked over at her aunt with an exaggerated look of innocence, "I'll do whatever my good and kind and loving aunt would like me to."

Feigning a gag, Melissa laughed, "Yes, sure you will."

They all laughed and sat back down at the table.

"We were just trying to figure out dinner," Melissa said.

Grace waved her hand, "You two do whatever you like, I'm going to make a quick sandwich and go upstairs to finish unpacking and then I'm going to bed."

She was really tired from all the driving and wanted to get a good night's sleep. They hadn't discussed when she would start work but Grace figured it would be on Monday.

"Oh," Melissa said, surprised.

Grace watched Melissa and John exchange glances and was glad she bowed out of dinner. They needed some time alone.

Excusing herself, Grace went over to the refrigerator and got out the fixings for her sandwich.

A few minutes later, Melissa and John got up and said they were going out for dinner.

When Grace was alone, she sat down at the table and ate her sandwich in silence. It was nice to just sit there and not think of anything.

Of course that wasn't what was happening, Grace's mind started thinking about her aunt and John. They seemed so cute!

Then that thought led to another cowboy..... The one who kissed her four years ago and then dumped her like a bag of trash.

Anger rode through Grace's chest like a spear. Sitting back, she played with the napkin she was using while wondering why TJ's dismissal was so heart-wrenching.

'Maybe,' she said to herself, 'because the kiss was the most exciting thing to ever happen to you.'

Frustrated by her thoughts, Grace got up and threw away her plate and shredded napkin.

Now was not the time to dwell on ancient history. After all, she thought as she walked back upstairs, she was grown up now. A kiss would have to be pretty earth-shattering to impress her nowadays.

Once she was upstairs, Grace sat on the bed and couldn't seem to get her body to do what she needed it to. Her mind just kept drifting back to that night at the hang out when he called her a kid and drove off.

Her phone ringing brought Grace back to the present. She looked at the screen and saw it was her brother, Brad, calling.

"Hey there," Grace said brightly.

Brad smiled, "I see you made it," he answered.

Grace chuckled, "Yes, I told you I would."

"You did," Brad said, then added, "I hope you have a really good time down there Grace."

Something in her brother's tone made Grace frown. He sounded worried. Very un-Brad-like in her opinion. Not that her brother didn't care about her, he did, it was just that Brad was the positive and care-free type normally.

"Are you worried that I won't?" Grace asked her brother.

Brad snorted, "No, I'm sure you will."

He paused then said, "It's just that you haven't wanted to go back down there and I know something happened."

Surprised, Grace didn't know what to say. She always thought she did such a good job of hiding her broken heart. She should have known Brad would see through her façade.

Grace pasted a smile back on her face before she responded, "Thank you Brad, I intend to have a very good time."

She thought he believed her since he changed the subject. They talked a few minutes more and ended the call with Grace promising to call him in a week or so to give a status.

After hanging up, Grace actually did get to work putting the rest of her things away. She tucked the bags up into the attic and was coming down the fold out stairs when she heard her aunt's front door open.

"Grace," Melissa called out.

Coming downstairs, a smile on her face, Grace looked at her aunt expectantly.

She laughed when Melissa just shook her head.

It was sweet to see her aunt blush.

"I said I wanted details," Grace said over her shoulder as she walked into the kitchen ahead of her aunt.

Melissa laughed, "And so you did," she answered but didn't say anything else.

Grace grabbed a bottled water and offered one to her aunt. When Melissa shook her head to decline it, Grace put it back and sat at the breakfast bar.

Sighing, Melissa sat down beside her. "What do you want to know?" She asked, resignation in her voice.

Trying not to laugh, Grace clamped her lips shut.

Play slapping at Grace, Melissa whined, "Come on, cut me some slack here."

"Okay," Grace laughed, "do you want to explain about the hot cowboy in your kitchen earlier?" She jokingly pushed against Melissa's shoulder.

Melissa rolled her eyes, "Fine, we've been dating for a while," she mumbled.

Grace's eyes widened, "And?" She asked expectantly.

Shaking her head, Melissa was embarrassed and asked, "What?"

Geez, it was like getting information out of a detainee.

"I want to know what he's like," Grace said in a sly voice. "You know," She wiggled her eyebrows, "is he a good kisser?"

Melissa pushed away from the table and started walking around the kitchen, "He's……" she sighed, "he's just John."

Grace nodded, "You're lack of answer says a lot."

Laughing, Melissa sat back down, "I know," she absently traced her finger in a circle on the tabletop, "It's just so……."

Having heard a similar description, or lack of description, from some of her friends, Grace knew that the relationship was pretty serious. At least her aunt thought so.

It was weird thinking of Melissa with someone. Grace cocked her head and studied her aunt.

"I know," Melissa said, "the confirmed bachelorette has fallen."

Not sure if that was the way she would put it, Grace shook her head in denial. "No," She said to her aunt.

Melissa looked at her, surprised by Grace's tone.

"I just meant," Grace began, "that it's not a bad thing."

They sat there for a few minutes, not saying anything, just staring into space.

Finally, Melissa broke the silence. "You know, you never told me why you wouldn't come back down here."

The one conversation Grace didn't want to have was now put out into the room.

Shaking her head, Grace sat up straighter, "I told you, I had college and stuff with my friends."

It was a lame excuse and Grace was a little ashamed of herself for using it.

"I always thought I was one of your friends," Melissa said.

Hearing the obvious hurt in her aunt's voice made Grace's chest hurt.

Grace turned to Melissa and hugged her. "You were and are my friend." Grace said, trying to reassure her aunt.

Melissa pulled away and looked at her niece, "Then why wouldn't you come back?" Starting to cry, she asked, "Did I do something that upset you?"

"Oh No!" Grace answered in a rush. "It was nothing you did, it was something someone else did."

The admission made Grace feel awful. She should have told her aunt back then but was too embarrassed.

Melissa became angry, "Who did what to you?" She demanded.

Oh great, Grace thought, now her aunt thought it was something really bad.

Sighing, Grace knew the whole story needed to come out.

"It wasn't like that, Auntie," Grace began telling her story.

Saying the words out loud to Melissa was more difficult than Grace expected it would be but she got through it. She explained the kiss and the run in with the boy a few days later.

After she got out the story, Grace felt silly. Looking back at it now, as an adult, it seemed really immature. But at the time, it was unbearably painful.

When Grace was done telling the story, she waited for her aunt to comment.

Melissa wasn't sure if she was more upset with her niece for keeping this from her or the jerk of a boy who made Grace feel so awful. This was a situation that could have been resolved a long time ago if only Grace would've talked to her.

"Well," Melissa finally said, "I'd like to give that boy a piece of my mind, that's for sure."

Grace couldn't help it, she giggled. Her aunt's defensiveness was so sweet. "Me too."

Getting up from the table, Melissa went over and turned on the oven, "Well," she said to her niece, "let's make some cookies and figure out the best revenge."

That was a fantastic idea as far as Grace was concerned.

"You got it," Grace responded as she hopped down from the table to help her aunt.

Chapter 4

The next day was Sunday so Grace spent the day doing errands with her aunt and re-acquainting herself with Lake Jackson.

Luckily the changes were small from the last time she was here. The biggest one was the construction of a bypass that allowed cars to avoid the incessant stop lights. Grace could appreciate that.

They stopped in at the office so Melissa could give Grace a little tour. After that, they got lunch at a local sports bar that served really good food. Grace loved the large tv screens on the walls.

On the way back to Melissa's house, Grace's phone rang. Since she was driving, she asked Melissa to answer it.

The caller was Raelynn, who wanted to welcome Grace back to town. Melissa was being sassy on the phone with her friend, which made Grace laugh.

"My niece is currently being my chauffer so she's not available to talk to knocked up women," Melissa said flippantly into the phone.

Melissa put the phone on speaker.

Raelynn's voice came out loud, "Don't listen to your aunt, Grace, she's just bitter."

Grace laughed, "I know, Raelynn."

"Hey," Melissa shouted, "don't pick on me!"

Raelynn laughed, "But it's so much fun," she said.

Grace shook her head, these two were very weird but adorable.

"Anyway," Raelynn said, "I wanted to invite the two of you over to ride on Tuesday." She paused, "And I know your aunt's schedule is light that day."

Melissa shook her head, "You don't have to ask me twice, I'll take you up on any chance to see my man."

Rolling her eyes, Grace pretended to be appalled by her aunt's words.

"Don't I know it," Raelynn shouted, "so we'll see you for lunch on Tuesday and then you can go riding." She added, "I'm sure John would love to be your escort."

Melissa was smiling and making goo-goo eyes at Grace, which made her laugh.

Grace stopped at a light and said, "We'll be there, can't wait to see you."

"Us too sweetie," Raelynn answered.

Melissa hung up the phone and placed it back in the cup holder between them.

Nodding to the phone, Grace said, "You two are something else."

Turning up the radio, Melissa smiled, "Yes we are."

A little ball of jealousy started up in Grace's mind. She pushed it away since it was silly to be jealous of someone else's good fortune.

As if sensing the change in Grace's mood, Melissa stopped joking and looked out the window.

Grace didn't want to bring her aunt down just because she had her own issues so she cleared her throat and smiled.

"I was just wishing that I had someone like you have Raelynn." Grace said a little wistfully.

Melissa felt sorry for Grace and she wished, again, that they hadn't had the last four years apart. It may not have made a difference but they would never know now.

Melissa reached over and squeezed Grace's hand that was resting between them, "I'm sorry, sweetie," she said.

"I know," Grace answered, "It's nothing you did though and I'll get over it."

Hearing the conviction in Grace's voice made Melissa feel better. They were so much alike.

They stopped at a light and Grace turned to look at her aunt.

Melissa kissed her niece on the cheek, "I'll help," she said brightly.

Grace figured that was just what she needed right now.

On Monday morning, Grace was up early and went to work with Melissa.

The office was already awake when they arrived. Melissa introduced Grace to her two interns from the nearby college.

"I'm Amy," The young woman said quietly.

Grace smiled and thought Amy was shy and awkward but pretty so she would probably turn into a stunner by the time she graduated college.

The young man stepped up and smiled big as he said, "I'm Brandon."

Sticking out her hand, Grace said, "I'm Grace, nice to meet you."

"The pleasure is all mine," Brandon replied.

Grace wasn't sure but it felt like there was a flirty undertone in his voice. She'd reserve judgment about him until she knew him better.

Melissa took her back to the offices and settled her into Raelynn's.

"I feel like I'm cheating on her," Melissa teased.

Cocking her head, Grace chuckled, "I'm sure," she said dryly.

Melissa pulled out some files and set them on the desk.

Grace was shown what to review the files for and how to re-file them.

Two hours later she was wondering how she would be able to do this all summer.

She really had to focus or all the numbers just sort of blurred together. It was very tedious, but it was necessary work that had to be done.

Getting up to stretch out, Grace went into the little kitchen area reserved for employees. She grabbed a soda out of the fridge, hoping some caffeine would help her wake up.

Brandon came in as she took a sip of the soda. He stood in the doorway looking at her with a cocky smile on his face.

'Oh, Hell no,' Grace thought to herself. 'This guy thought he actually stood a chance. Pity he was so delusional.'

Without even saying anything, Grace smiled sweetly and left the break room.

Melissa came in at lunchtime and asked Grace if she wanted to get lunch.

Grace didn't need to be asked twice. She was famished.

"So," Melissa asked as they got into her car, "how's it going?"

Frowning, Grace wasn't sure if she should be honest or not. Her aunt didn't give her a chance to decide before she interrupted.

"It's like wading through oatmeal right?" Melissa asked and tried not to laugh at the look on Grace's face.

Grace laughed. "Yes."

They got into Melissa's car and drove to a nearby restaurant. There was a buffet so they could each pick what they wanted with virtually no waiting.

After loading up a plate with salad, because she didn't want to feel guilty, Grace sat down and waited for her aunt before digging into her lunch.

"Salad?" Melissa asked when she sat down.

Nodding, Grace frowned, "I'm not going to balloon up and go crazy down here."

Melissa laughed. "I doubt that could happen. You're as skinny as a twig."

Funny that her aunt thought that because Grace certainly didn't. She always thought of herself as average.

Of course, compared to her aunt, most people were average. In Grace's eyes, her aunt was gorgeous.

She had long dark, curly hair that always looked full and beautiful.   Her makeup was light but looked very polished. She always wore sharp clothes that Grace was pretty sure were shown on runways in New York.

"I'm not but thank you," Grace said dryly.

Melissa put her fork down and looked at her niece intensely before saying. "Grace, we never see ourselves as others do, it's a matter of just being okay with who you see in the mirror at the end of the day."

Grace reminded herself to put "wise" on the list of her aunt's attributes.

She looked at her aunt and smiled, "I will try."

"That's all we can ask for," Melissa answered and picked up her fork again to eat.

The rest of the meal was nice. They chatted about work and the weather and the horseback riding they were going to do tomorrow.

On the way back to the office, Grace was absently looking out the window of the car to let the sunlight shine on her face. It felt good to be outside so the thought of going back to work was just this side of depressing.

Surprisingly, the afternoon passed really quickly and Grace was deep in a file when Melissa came into the office and announced it was quitting time.

Grace straightened up the desk and dutifully marked the place she stopped at in the current file she was working on.

They left the office after everyone else since Melissa had to lock up.

In the car, Melissa asked, "How was your first day?"

Considering that her aunt was not further than about twenty-five feet from her all day and they had lunch together, Grace was confused.

"Um, it was fine," Grace said slowly.

Laughing, Melissa got in the car and started it up. "I'm just making conversation here with my carpool buddy."

It was hard to not laugh with her aunt's infectious humor, "I'm sure," she said flippantly.

They drove home with the music turned up and joked about some of the goings on at work.

"Oh yeah," Melissa said, "How's Brandon treating you?"

Grace actually huffed out a breath. "I can see that he's never been told no."

Melissa laughed, "He's a good looking guy but a little too self-promotional," she said as she pulled into the driveway.

"That's a polite way of putting it," Grace responded and opened up her car door.

They got out of the vehicle and walked up to the house.

After unlocking the door, Melissa tossed her briefcase onto the entryway table and walked into the kitchen.

Grace went upstairs to change.

When she came downstairs a few minutes later, she heard voices in the kitchen. Funny, she didn't hear anyone come in.

As she entered the kitchen, she saw Melissa at the table with John. Was the guy a ninja? He didn't make a sound when he came in.

Grace stood in the doorway and watched the couple. It was sweet to see her aunt that wrapped up in someone else. A pang of envy dropped into her chest but she quickly squelched it. She should just be happy for her aunt.

Clearing her throat, to announce her presence, Grace said cheerfully, "Hey John, how are you?"

The way John tensed at the sound of Grace's voice, and blushed like he was caught doing something he shouldn't, was almost comical.

"Uh, Grace," John murmured, "I'm fine, how are you?"

When he tipped his head in Grace's direction as an acknowledgement, she blushed a little. He was definitely a gentleman.

Grace went to the sink and poured herself a glass of water, "I'm great, my boss is a little bit of a tyrant, but I'll muddle through."

Ducking to avoid the dish towel Melissa tossed her way, Grace laughed. "I'll leave you to for a little bit, I'm going for a run."

Melissa frowned, "Oh sweetie, you don't have to go."

Smiling, Grace nodded toward the door, "Yes, I run pretty regularly and took a few days off for the trip so I need to get back out there."

She took a sip of water, set the glass on the counter, and went out to the front porch to stretch out.

A few minutes later, Grace was off to a slow jog to warm up. She actually hated exercising but knew it was mandatory if she wanted to eat what she liked.

Once she was warmed up, she started to increase her pace. It was nice, running through the neighborhood her aunt lived in. The houses were a bit older but everyone took such pride in their yards that it was nice to look at.

The front doors were adorned with wreaths in bright fall colors. One house had a fantastic fall display set up complete with bales of hay and life-sized scarecrows.

Even in the early evening, with the sun setting quickly, it was nice to run. The weather down here was so much milder than up in Virginia.

By the time she got back to Melissa's house, Grace felt better. The run helped her push out the doubts she let gather up during the day.

When she entered the house, she expected to see Melissa. "Hello?," She yelled down the hallway.

Getting no answer, she went into the kitchen to find a note on the table from her aunt.

Grace:

John and I went out to dinner and to a movie. Please help yourself to a casserole in the fridge.

Love you.

Being thrown over for a guy wasn't the end of the world but it did sting a bit.

'Oh well,' Grace thought, 'worse things could happen.'

She went to the refrigerator in search of some dinner.

Chapter 5

Tuesday morning, Grace woke up happy. They were going to go horseback riding today. Whoo hoo! She practically jumped out of bed and went into the bathroom to get ready.

She loved horses since her aunt first took her when she was about ten. It was so much fun to ride fast. Luckily, every summer, Melissa took Grace out almost every week.

Most girls developed a love affair with horses but Grace was able to realize hers. When she went home to her parents' house, they agreed to get her lessons.

After getting ready, Grace practically floated down the stairs and into the kitchen where her aunt was hovering over the coffee maker.

"Good morning," Grace said cheerfully.

Melissa looked up and smiled, "You're cheerful this morning."

Grace nodded and said, "Two reasons, one.." she held up a finger, "we're getting off of work early, and two," she held up another finger, "I get to ride."

Melissa chuckled and remembered how Grace always loved riding.

"Well," Melissa smiled slyly, "that's good because I got you a little welcome back gift."

Her eyebrows raised, Grace followed her aunt

into the living room, curious about what the gift could be.

Melissa pulled out two large boxes from behind a chair and handed them to her niece.

Grace was giddy with excitement. She loved surprises.

Taking the boxes from her aunt, Grace plopped down on the floor and set one box on her lap and the other to one side.

Opening the box, Grace gasped. Inside was a black cowboy hat. Not just a cowboy hat, but a blinged out one complete with a band of crystals and some lace with more crystals on the sides.

"Oh my," Grace whispered and placed the hat on her head.

Grace jumped up and went over to a wall mirror to look at the hat. It fit her head perfectly and made her look like a cowgirl with flair.

She spun around and made a pose with one hip jutting out.

Melissa clapped, she was relieved it fit and even more relieved that Grace liked it.

"One more," Melissa said and pointed to the other box.

Grace jumped in excitement, "Oh yeah," she said and ran back to where the other box was.

She grabbed the top and pulled it up. Inside were a pair of cowboy boots that were perfect.

Pulling them out, Grace was almost screeching with child-like excitement.

"They're gorgeous," She said brightly to her aunt.

Smiling, Melissa hugged her niece, "I hoped you would like them."

Grace looked at her aunt shockingly, "LIKE? I love them!"

As she pulled the boots out of the box, she oohed and aahed over them. They were black but had little cutouts of hearts all down the shaft and over the toe. The hearts were done in different shades of pink and purple. The boots were crazy, girlie, but Grace didn't care.

Looking up at her aunt, Grace slipped the boots on and stood up. She walked around the room posing and dancing, prompting a good amount of whooping from Melissa.

Once the initial excitement was over, Grace looked at the clock and realized they had to get a move on for work so she took off the boots and put them back in the box. The hat was next.

After eating a quick breakfast, the girls took the boxes plus clothes they would wear for the ride and put them in the back of the car.

Melissa drove them to work and they each walked in with huge smiles on their faces.

Grace was so glad they were only working a half day today because she was too excited to focus for a full day.

At 11:30am she was enmeshed in a complicated file when Melissa knocked on the doorframe of the office.

"Hey there, this is your thirty minute warning," Melissa said brightly.

Nodding, Grace smiled and went back to her file. She thought if she focused, she might get the review done and notes taken.

A few minutes later, Brandon was standing in the doorway. His presence made the hair on Grace's nape stand up so she looked up at him. There was something about him that made her slightly uneasy.

Frowning, Grace asked, "Is there something you need?"

The look on his face was disgusting as far as Grace was concerned. It looked like he wanted to say something vulgar but, luckily for him, he refrained.

"I was just wondering if you wanted to have lunch with me." Brandon said slowly.

Grace was going to answer when Melissa showed up behind Brandon.

"Excuse me," Melissa said sternly, "I'm taking my niece out for the afternoon."

Brandon's face looked mortified and Grace wanted to laugh. 'There,' she thought, 'you deserved that.'

Smiling sweetly, Grace put away her file and got up to join her aunt.

When they were outside, Melissa turned to face Grace and asked, "What was that about?"

Shrugging, Grace answered, "I guess he thinks he has a chance."

Melissa laughed. "I'm assuming he doesn't by your tone."

Grace nodded, "Not a chance in hell." She responded and got into the car.

They didn't talk about the lustful Brandon anymore.

Watching out the window, Grace enjoyed the views here. They were going north on Highway 288. There were rows of trees and fields along the roadway that, even this late in the year, were still green.

The sun was shining and the air was mild. 'A perfect day for riding,' Grace thought.

Melissa turned the car off of the main highway onto FM 1462 east.

"Alvin," Grace said to her aunt when she read the sign.

"We're not going all the way there, Seth's ranch is just a few miles down this road." She said to Grace as they sped up.

Fence posts were passing by and the scenery before her was serene. Grace thought this was about as good as it got for playing hooky from work.

A few minutes down the road, Melissa turned off the highway onto a gravel driveway. There was a huge gate with a giant SS on the top of it.

Grace asked, "What does the SS stand for?"

Melissa's lips set grimly, she said, "I guess Seth was engaged when he bought the ranch so the SS stands for Seth and Sam, which was her name."

Forming a silent "O" with her lips, Grace didn't ask anything else. The tone of her aunt's voice told her that this Sam person was a sore subject.

Turning her attention back out the window, Grace looked out over the Texas landscape.

The ranch seemed endless, she could see fences stretched out into the distance. There were cattle grazing in the fields and, as they neared a gathering of buildings, she could see horses.

Just seeing the beautiful animals made Grace happy. Some of her best memories were of riding.

As soon as Melissa put the vehicle in park, Grace was out and going to the back to get her boots and hat out.

Melissa grabbed a bag with their change of clothes and they headed over to the barn.

Grace could smell hay and horses. The fall breezes blew gently. She was in Heaven.

"Hey there!" John called out from the entryway of the barn.

Grace walked up and shook John's hand and then stepped back, sure that Melissa would hug and kiss him.

Melissa smiled and said, "Hi."

John didn't make a move toward her, only smiled and tipped his hat.

Grace was confused. They acted like a couple at her aunt's house, but here, there was distance. John turned to walk into the barn and motioned them to follow him.

Looking at her aunt, Grace had the question in her eyes. Melissa only nodded and glared as if to say, 'I'll tell you later.'

About halfway through the huge structure they stopped in front of some stalls.

John turned and looked at Grace. "How much experience riding have you had?" He asked.

"A good amount," Grace said and looked into the stall. "I rode every summer as a kid and volunteered at a rescue the last couple of years."

Her answer seemed to appease him thankfully.

John slid open one of the stall doors and stepped in for a second. When he came out, he was leading a painted pony.

Grace stepped back to allow the man and horse room to step into the barn's corridor.

"Oh," Grace whispered as the pony came around and faced her.

She was beautiful, with mostly a white coat with beautiful brown designs. Grace's breath hitched as she tentatively reached up and scratched the pony's forehead.

John smiled, "This is Cinderella," he said and laughed at the look on Grace's face.

Grace looked from her aunt to John then back to the pony.

"But we just call her Cindy," John spoke as he led the horse out toward the back of the barn.

She followed the horse and John blindly, as if they were the pied pipers.

Frowning, Grace turned to look at Melissa, "Where's your horse?" She asked.

Melissa smiled and nodded off to a small ring to the right of the barn. "She's in there," Melissa said.

John handed the reins to Grace to hold while he brushed Cindy.

Grace murmured sweet words to the pony and scratched behind her ears while John prepped her for the saddle.

Melissa stood a few feet away and watched her niece fall in love with the pony.

She jumped when she felt a hand on her shoulder and turned around quickly. Seeing Raelynn behind her, she smiled and grabbed her friend for a hug.

"Hello there," Raelynn said as her friend squeezed her tightly.

Melissa pulled back and asked, "Why do you have to look so damn beautiful?"

Raelynn laughed at her friend's outrageous declaration. "I guess because I'm lucky," She answered.

Grace looked over and noticed Raelynn talking to her aunt. "Raelynn!" She yelled and jogged over.

"Grace," Raelynn said as she gathered the girl into her arms. It was tough to hug with her protruding belly.

After hugging Raelynn, Grace stepped back and immediately put her hands on the now big, belly.

Her eyes widened, "Holy cow," Grace said, "what do you have in there?" She asked.

Raelynn smiled and answered, "I think there are ten of them in there sometimes but the doctor says only one."

"Where's Seth?" Melissa asked. "I'd like Grace to meet him."

Looking around, Raelynn shrugged, "I'm not sure actually," she smiled, "he had a meeting with one of the neighboring ranchers but said he'd be back soon."

Nodding, Melissa looked over at John. He was just finishing up saddling Grace's mount.

"Well, I'd better get Lucy ready," Melissa said and walked over to the ring where the horse was standing.

Raelynn smiled at her friend then turned to face Grace, "So, how's it going?" She asked.

Grace bobbed her head from side to side, "It's okay, not my particular cup of tea, but it's fine for now." She answered.

Nodding, Raelynn could empathize. "I know that reviewing the files and getting them ready for transferring into our new system is tedious. I don't envy you."

Glaring at Raelynn, Grace pointed and said, "So you deliberately got yourself pregnant to avoid doing files?" She cocked her head to consider it, "Very smart!"

Raelynn laughed. Grace always made her laugh. She was just like Melissa in that respect.

"I try," Raelynn said dryly.

Grace sobered her tone, "Are you happy?" She asked.

Nodding, Raelynn put her hands on her belly protectively, "Immensely."

"Good," Grace said, then asked, "How does Hailey feel about the new brother or sister?"

They started walking toward the pen where Melissa and John were brushing down Lucy and talking.

Raelynn sighed, "She's happy for us but I think she's a little unsure where she fits in."

Grace felt bad for her friend Hailey, but had to ask, "Is that why she's in Europe?"

Knowing that Melissa told Grace everything, much like she herself did with Hailey, Raelynn wasn't offended by the question.

"I think that's part of it," Raelynn responded, "but she's been begging me for a couple of years now to let her go."

Grace pondered the information. "So," She said, "you got pregnant and she got what she wanted," sighing, she smirked. "Smart girl."

Raelynn laughed and rubbed Grace's back in a motherly touch.

As they got up closer, Grace could see her aunt and John having a kind of intimate conversation.

"Should we walk back?" Grace asked.

Shaking her head no, Raelynn smiled. "John is all, by-the-book cowboy when he's on the clock so he doesn't show much."

That explained why he didn't greet her aunt as warmly as she would've thought.

"I see," Grace said quietly.

A few minutes later, Melissa was leading her horse over to where Raelynn and Grace stood. They mounted up and started out down the path that lead away from the buildings.

Chapter 6

Grace and Melissa rode for a while, neither of them talking. It was enough to just ride and enjoy the weather.

Melissa was the first to break the comfortable silence when she asked, "Are you having fun?"

Feeling the breeze and sun on her skin, and feeling truly relaxed for the first time in a while, Grace nodded.

"John was going to come with us but I told him that we'd be fine on our own." Melissa said dryly. "Geez, like two grown women couldn't handle a horseback ride."

Laughing at her aunt's pretense at being offended, Grace answered, "I'm sure we can find some trouble to get into."

The twinkle in Grace's eyes made Melissa's heart swell. This was the little girl she remembered.

Grace clicked her tongue and moved her heels so that Cindy knew to pick up the pace. The increased motion made Grace's hair swirl around her shoulders and gave her a quick shot of exhilaration.

'This is what I need,' Grace said to herself.

After a few minutes, Melissa was beside her and when Grace looked over, she recognized the same challenge in her aunt's eyes as her own. Without saying anything, they both prodded their horses into a run.

Seth Rhodes arrived back at his ranch in his truck. He recognized Melissa's car parked by the house and smiled. 'Good,' he said to himself, 'Raelynn needed the company.'

As he got out and headed over to the barn, he noticed another truck coming up the driveway. He didn't recognize the vehicle so he stood where he was and waited.

Raelynn came out of the barn and saw her husband standing in the parking area.

"Hey there handsome," Raelynn called out to him.

Seth turned to see his wife making her way over to him and smiled. Lord she was a sight, the most beautiful woman in the world! Her hands were settled protectively over her expanding belly.

Knowing she carried his child gave him a feeling of pride. As much as he loved Hailey, he knew that she wouldn't want to run the ranch someday. This child, he was sure would have the rancher's blood in his or her veins and would carry it on.

"Hello there beautiful," Seth said when Raelynn was closer.

"Who's that?" Raelynn asked as she nodded toward the truck coming up the drive.

Seth shook his head, "Don't know yet," he answered and took her hand into his.

The truck was close enough that Seth could see the driver. He smiled.

Raelynn watched her husband's growing smile and asked, "You know him?"

Nodding, Seth responded, "Yep, my neighbor, Tavin."

Shrugging, Raelynn didn't know who that was. Even after living with Seth for the last year on the ranch, she still didn't know all the neighbors. Everyone was friendly but they were all so busy with their own places that they didn't get together often.

As the truck stopped, Raelynn watched the drive with curiosity as he got out.

"Tavin," Seth said with a smile, "how the hell are you?"

Smiling, Tavin walked over to his friend, "Seth, I'm good, how are you?" He looked at the lovely woman standing next to his friend, "And who is this?"

Raelynn blushed as the young man took her hand in his and gently kissed the back of it. He tipped his hat in her direction and said, "Ma'am."

A girl never got used to being fussed over by a man. Especially a good looking one.

Seth cleared his throat in a gesture of 'back off' and said, "Tavin, this is my wife, Raelynn."

Raelynn almost laughed at the look of pure astonishment that crossed Tavin's face.

"I'll be damned," Tavin whispered than looked chagrined, "Excuse my language ma'am."

Chuckling, Raelynn said, "It's okay Tavin," she looked at her husband, "Why don't I go inside and get you both something to drink?"

The two men watched Raelynn make her way into the house. When the door closed behind her, Tavin turned to his friend.

"Why didn't you tell me you got married?" He punched Seth in the shoulder to emphasize his point.

Seth pushed Tavin back good naturedly, "Check your damn mail, you got an invitation." He said loudly.

They headed toward the barn.

Tavin slapped his friend on the back, "Well from the look of your bride, you've been keeping her busy," Tavin said with a sly smile.

"I'm trying," Seth returned.

Once inside the barn, they headed toward the other end and out into the training area.

John was in one of the rings working with a gelding.

Seth and Tavin watched John as he worked with the animal. They would comment here and there about the horse but pretty much just stood there and watched as John tried to get the horse to follow his commands.

That's where they were still standing when Tavin noticed two horses coming from the east. They were coming in fast and he nudged Seth's arm.

"Hey, are they supposed to be riding like that?" Tavin asked.

Seth smiled, "That's Melissa, Raelynn's friend, and her niece." He looked over at Tavin then back to the two women, "They are harmless."

The race was on! And Grace was currently winning!

As the horses sped across the landscape, Grace was laughing and hollering, "Come on!"

Melissa was only a half-length behind her.

The buildings of the ranch were in sight now and they were getting bigger as the horses ran. She should be slowing down but she didn't really want to. Judging the distance, Grace figured they could go another quarter mile or so before they had to stop.

Tavin was getting anxious, the horses were coming in too fast and were too close to the buildings for his comfort. He looked at Seth but didn't say anything.

'Well,' Tavin thought, 'I'll step out and say something if he doesn't.'

The smile on Grace's face was huge. She loved the feeling of freedom. When she looked back she saw Melissa pull up on the reins to slow her horse down.

Realizing it was a smart idea and, even though she didn't want to, Grace pulled her reins in to start slowing Cindy down as well.

As she slowed to a cantor, she could see a man walking away from the paddock and into the area the horses were heading for.

Seth followed his friend, who was obviously, going to intercept the riders and tell them they were being careless riding the way they were.

Knowing Melissa the way he did, Seth wasn't worried. Her niece, from all accounts, was responsible so he didn't think they'd hurt themselves or anyone else.

'It's funny,' Seth thought to himself, 'that Tavin would worry about some ladies on horses when he traveled the rodeo circuit around the county doing crazy stuff like riding broncs and bulls.'

As Seth walked over to him, Tavin shot him a grimace.

Seth just shook his head and smiled.

Grace was slowing Cindy to a walk and was sad that the ride had to end so soon. She could hear her aunt yelling hello to Seth.

One of the two men in front of her waved so she figured he was Seth. She'd seen photos of him at her aunt's house but it was nice to know who to greet first.

The other man had his hat pulled down low so Grace couldn't see his face clearly.

Melissa caught up to her niece and they walked the horses the last hundred feet or so.

"Who's that with Seth?" Grace asked her aunt.

Squinting, Melissa shook her head, "I don't know, it's hard to see his face."

John walked up beside Tavin and Seth and smiled. He stepped forward to meet the ladies and their horses.

Pulling Cindy up to stop, Grace smiled as John took the reins from Melissa and helped her down off her horse.

Grace stayed in the saddle while John and Melissa led her horse to the barn to be brushed and cooled down.

Seth stepped forward, "You must be Grace," he said with a smile.

"And you must be Seth," Grace said back. She reached down and shook his hand quickly.

Deciding he liked Melissa's niece, Seth chuckled. He looked over at his friend. "Oh, please excuse my manners," He pointed behind him, "This is my neighbor, Tavin McCormick."

The word 'Tavin' sent bells off inside of Grace. Did she hear Seth right? She looked over just as the cowboy stepped forward and raised his hat so she could see his face.

It was him! Grace's heart was going as fast as her horse was just a few minutes earlier. Her eyes widened and her shoulders raised with every breath she took.

Tavin looked up into eyes he remembered from years earlier. The last time he saw them, they looked a lot like they did right now, wide and in shock.

Grace sat there looking at Tavin and didn't know what to say. What was he doing here? She searched her brain, 'Seth said he was a neighbor,' she recalled.

Clearing his throat, Tavin put his fingers to his hat and tipped it toward Grace, "Ma'am," he said in a calm voice that was in direct contradiction to how he felt.

Looking from Seth's smiling face to Tavin's shocked one, Grace didn't know what she should do.

He stood there and looked at her like it didn't matter. Like his actions and words didn't mean anything. Like he hadn't kissed her like he loved her and then discarded her like trash. The more she thought about it, the more anger she generated.

Without thinking about it, Grace jumped down off the horse. Because she was raised right, she looked at Seth and shook his hand.

"Thank you for letting us ride today, it was great," Grace said to Seth.

Seth smiled, "It was my pleasure, Cindy here doesn't get much use with Raelynn expecting so I'll bet she had as good of a time as you did."

Absently rubbing the pony's neck, Grace nodded at Seth's words. Even though her eyes weren't on him, she knew exactly where Tavin stood.

"I hope so," She responded and smiled as one of the ranch hands came up to take the pony away.

"I've got tea!" Raelynn hollered from the barn.

Seth nodded toward his wife, "Excuse me, I'm going to go and give her a hand."

Grace watched the nice man walk away. When she turned her head back, she was face to face with Tavin.

Tavin didn't say anything. He couldn't. It was her! It was the woman he thought about for 4 years. She was right in front of him and he couldn't say anything. She looked different, definitely grown up now.

"You," Grace said in a breathy voice.

Clearing his throat again, Tavin responded, "You."

Grace was definitely torn between anger and excitement. They stood right where they were and just stared at one another. It was like they were daring each other to make a move.

Seconds, or minutes, or hours passed. Grace didn't want to move but she couldn't stay and watch him look at her that way. Finally, the tension was too much and she stepped forward.

Lifting her palms, she placed each of them on both of his cheeks. The stubble from his whiskers tickled her palms and caused a delightful friction against her skin.

Taking another step closer, Grace looked up into his eyes. They were a blue-green color that grew darker as she moved in.

Closing her eyes, Grace reached up and touched her lips to his. The initial touch was electrifying, jolting sensation after sensation through her body.

Tavin was lost, he didn't move his arms, just stood there and let her kiss him. His body was screaming at him to respond but he was lost in a haze of confusion and want.

Grace thought the kiss was very similar to the one they shared years before, only this time he didn't move his hands over her body. She was in control this time around, she took him by surprise this time.

Gently pulling back, Grace smiled up into Tavin's eyes. They were wide and filled with bewilderment. 'Good,' she thought. He deserved to wonder what the hell was going on. Lord knew she did back then.

Grace stepped back, still smiling, and pulled her hand back. Without giving him time to say anything, she hauled off and smacked him across the face. The "Thwack," the action made was loud.

When she turned around to walk away, Grace found four sets of eyes starting at her.

Chapter 7

Grace stopped and looked at Melissa, John, Raelynn, and Seth. Melissa's mouth was hanging open in shock while the other three just looked puzzled.

"I'll let him explain," Grace said nonchalantly and walked into the barn.

All four eyes turned to focus on Tavin.

His cheek still stinging from Grace's slap, Tavin turned around to look at his neighbors. 'Oh great,' he thought to himself. 'How do I explain this one?'

Seth gained his composure first, "Uh, do you want to explain that?" He asked Tavin.

Melissa spoke up then, the situation clearing in her mind, "You're him," she said while pointing at Tavin, "You're the guy who kissed her then made her feel like garbage!"

John sensed his lady's anger and stepped forward to defend her, "Boy, you'd better explain yourself or I'll whoop your butt and then kick you off of this land!"

Knowing John never said anything he didn't mean, Tavin nodded. "Okay, okay."

He walked over to the group, "Grace and I shared a kiss a couple of years back and when I found out she was still a kid, I told her I couldn't see her," he looked, and felt, guilty about his actions even now.

"No!" Melissa shouted, "You weren't all nice, you were mean and cruel!" She took a breath, "And you made her not want to come back down here for 4 years!"

Seth stepped forward, "Is that true Tavin?" He asked.

Raelynn was confused but got the gist of what was going on. "Let's all calm down, we don't know what happened exactly," she said, trying to be diplomatic.

"If you want to listen to him, that's fine," Melissa shot back, "I'm going to check on my niece."

John stood there and didn't know if he should beat the boy or go after Melissa.

Tavin watched Melissa leave and looked back at his friends, "Seth, I didn't know that what I said made her so mad." He nodded in the direction Grace and Melissa went, "I kissed her and then found out she was too young. I was embarrassed."

Shaking her head, Raelynn frowned, "I'm sure you thought it was okay but obviously, from Grace's perspective, you were cruel."

"And I'm sorrier about that ma'am than I can ever say." Tavin answered.

John piped up, "It don't matter boy! You hurt that little girl."

Seth was afraid John would tear into Tavin so he turned to his foreman, "John, why don't you go and check on Melissa and Grace."

After John nodded and left, Seth turned back to Tavin. "What were you thinking?" He asked his friend.

The three of them walked over to the fence. There was a bench nearby so Seth helped Raelynn sit down. They looked back at Tavin and waited for his explanation.

"I saw her around town and thought she was pretty." Tavin began. "I ran into her at a party down by the lake and we kissed." He blushed a little at talking in front of a lady, "A few days later I ran into her and Hailey in town and found out she was still in high school."

The situation was becoming clearer but didn't sit well with Seth.

Tavin could see his friend's reaction, "I know," he said, "I was 27 at the time and I panicked."

Raelynn spoke up, "How did you know Hailey?"

Looking at Seth's wife, Tavin smiled. "I did some volunteer work at the high school and she was in one of the FFA classes I helped out in."

Nodding, Raelynn sat back and listened.

"Honestly, Seth, I didn't know what I said had that much of an effect on her." Tavin said, feeling low.

"She got a good one in," Seth answered and pointed at Tavin's cheek. "Still red."

Absently rubbing his cheek, Tavin smiled. "Yep, she did."

Even being around Seth a lot, Raelynn couldn't figure out why either of the men was smiling. This situation was not something to smile about. She decided to go and find out if Grace was alright.

Grace stood next to her aunt's car and tried to catch her breath. How could she have kissed him? And more incredibly, how could she have slapped him like that?

Her aunt walked out of the barn and headed toward her. A few minutes later, Grace saw John coming her way too.

"Are you okay?" Melissa asked when she reached her niece.

Grace nodded, "Yes," she answered and added, "I'm sorry if my actions embarrassed you."

Melissa looked shocked, "Are you kidding me? I thought it was brilliant!"

John finally joined them. "Are you ladies okay?" He asked.

Grace thought he was so sweet, "Yes, we're fine."

"Did you want me to run him off?" John asked Grace in a serious voice.

She couldn't help it, Grace laughed, "No," she answered, "I'm sorry if my actions upset you."

John stepped forward, "Your aunt is my lady, and since you are her family, you're mine too." He smiled at Melissa, "I won't have some buck come around and make you feel bad."

It was easy to imagine John on a ranch a hundred or two hundred years earlier saying the exact same thing. He was such a nice man.

"I'm fine, really," Grace responded. "Do you need me to apologize to Seth or Raelynn?" She asked her aunt.

Melissa shook her head, "I don't think so, it's not like you go around doing that kind of stuff." She stopped and asked, "Do you?"

They all laughed.

Grace looked at her boots and up into her aunt's still-worried face, "Not usually," She said dryly.

"Good," Melissa answered.

They were still standing by the car talking a while later, when they saw Raelynn walking over to them.

Grace was ready to say she was sorry when Raelynn held up her hand, "Don't even say you're sorry, you have nothing to be sorry for." She said.

Melissa winked at Raelynn. "See, I told you," She said to her niece.

"Did he explain?" Melissa asked Raelynn.

Nodding, Raelynn looked at John, "Seth asked if you wanted to come back and finish with the horse as long as you weren't going to wear the tar out of the boy." She smiled, "His words not mine."

John smiled, "Nah, he gets off easy today," he answered. After tipping his hats to the ladies, he headed back over to the barn.

"Well," Melissa started, "we should get going; we've caused enough excitement for one day."

Raelynn's smile faded, "I guess."

Melissa hugged her friend, "We'll stop by tomorrow after work; I've got some stuff for you to look at anyway."

Hugging her friend, Raelynn said, "Okay."

"Hey," Melissa glared at Raelynn, "why aren't you in bed?"

Looking at Grace, Raelynn tried to look innocent, "I was just up for a little bit."

Melissa shook her head, "You're lucky I'm not your doctor."

"I'm sure," Raelynn smiled over brightly.

The women got into the car and waved to Raelynn as they left the ranch.

Tavin felt like Seth was convinced of his sincerity in the misunderstanding with Grace. However, John was still pissed and Tavin could understand why. If it would have been some guy making his sister hurt, he would've ripped the jackass' arms off and beat him with them. Hopefully John didn't want to do that.

A while later, Tavin and Seth were walking out to Tavin's truck so he could get back to his own place.

"Can I ask you something?" Seth questioned his friend.

Tavin nodded, "Sure," he said.

Seth looked around, not sure why he was asking the question. "Why did you kiss her?"

Confused, Tavin answered with his own question, "Then or now?"

Smirking, Seth answered, "Then."

That was the question of the hour in Tavin's own mind. "I saw her around, you know," He said and waited for Seth to nod before he said, "I don't know exactly, she was just pretty and I wanted to touch her and kiss her."

Saying the words out loud made Tavin shameful. He didn't know what else to say.

Seth interrupted his thoughts, "And how did you feel today?"

Tavin wondered if his neighbor was going to become a counselor. "Why the questions?" He asked Seth as he got into his truck.

"Just wondering," Seth answered. "The first time Raelynn kissed me I thought the ground was being pulled out from under my feet." He looked around, a little embarrassed for admitting things. "I was just wondering if you felt the same way."

After starting up his truck, Tavin turned to look at his friend, "Yep," He said and pulled away.

Seth smiled and watched his friend drive down the driveway. Raelynn walked up to him and put her arm around his back.

"Everything okay?" Raelynn asked her husband.

Looking over at his beautiful wife, Seth answered, "Yes."

They walked into the house together.

Melissa pulled into the driveway of her place and put the car in park. Grace was surprisingly quiet the entire ride home and Melissa feared her niece was really thrown by today's run in with Tavin McCormick.

What could she say to Grace? Could she offer any useful advice in this situation? Probably not and that made Melissa even more upset. She should be able to help her niece. They got out of the car and into the house before she spoke.

"I feel bad that I can't help you." She said to Grace.

Grace shook her head, "Auntie, you don't have to. I'm an adult and I'll figure this out." She sighed.

Melissa nodded, "Well, if you need any help, I'm here," She said.

Getting some food from the refrigerator, Grace smiled, "I know."

They made dinner in silence. It was just a salad with some chicken thrown in but it was easy and good.

After clearing the table and washing the few dishes they used, Grace was standing at the sink when she started laughing.

Melissa looked at her, confused, "Are you okay?" She asked.

"I was just thinking of the look on his face when I slapped him," Grace said through her laughter.

Joining in, Melissa started to laugh, "I know, we were all standing there and we saw you kiss him and were like, "What." Then when you slapped him, it was like, "WHAT!"

"I'll bet," Grace said to her aunt.

Melissa shook her head, "You did what you thought you had to in order to get your point across."

Glad her aunt could see her reasoning, Grace smiled. "I know, I guess I was just surprised at myself."

"Who knows why we react the way we do." Melissa said.

Grace sat down at the table and thought about what her aunt said, "Why did I kiss him today?" She asked.

Melissa shook her head, "I'm not sure," she answered. "But, how was it?"

That question was not one that Grace could easily answer. She didn't want to admit that the second her lips touched his that her body went into a tailspin of excitement. It was difficult to express that her heart wanted to beat out of her chest and she would've given anything to have Tavin pull her to him and kiss her like he did years earlier.

Pulling herself out of her dream-like state, Grace looked at her aunt, "It was amazing but, like before, only one-sided."

"Don't be so sure," Melissa said quickly.

Her aunt's statement made Grace's head snap up. "What do you mean?" She asked.

"You know that I'm dating a cowboy right?" Melissa asked smartly. "Well, cowboys tend to be a little different breed of men."

Grace was lost.

Melissa placed her hand over her niece's. "I can't really speak for Tavin since I only want to kick his butt for hurting you," she smiled, "but if his face said anything, it said that he was affected by the kiss."

That one sentence gave Grace a mixture of satisfaction and hope.

"I guess we'll see." Grace said and got up from the table to go up to her room.

Chapter 8

A week later, Grace was sitting in Raelynn's office and still thinking about that stupid kiss.

She spent every available moment thinking about Tavin and that kiss and that slap. It was to the point where she couldn't focus on anything for more than a few minutes. It was downright annoying!

Even the notoriously pestering Brandon didn't get to her. He asked her to go out with him on a daily basis now and she basically ignored him.

The file she was working on was thick and contained a lot of information. This was the fourth time she was reading through it because she was afraid she'd missed something with being distracted.

When her aunt came into the office, Grace sat back and was relieved for the distraction.

Melissa looked at her niece and felt sorry for her. It was clear that the situation with Tavin was not sitting well with her.

"How's it going?" Melissa asked in a hopeful tone.

Grace smiled back and said, "I'm trying."

That was clear to Melissa. Unfortunately, trying wasn't going to get the situation resolved.

"Raelynn called," Melissa said. "She wanted to check up on you and ask if we wanted to come out tomorrow for riding."

The thought of riding, although appealing, made Grace wonder if she had to worry about running into Tavin.

It wasn't difficult for Melissa to see the thoughts running through her niece's mind. "I was assured that he's out of town."

Grace shook her head, "You two are awesome!" She said.

"We are," Melissa answered. "We could probably rule the country if we were given the chance."

Her aunt's humor was contagious. "I'll bet." She answered.

Melissa stood up, "Okay, back to work!" She tried to sound stern but failed.

Grace called after her, "Aye, Aye Captain."

Work went smoother after that. Grace thought maybe it was because she knew Tavin was gone.

Tavin......she said his name in her head. It was an unusual name that was for sure. How did he get it? Was it a family name?

'Those questions will get you nowhere,' Grace said to herself.

She got through the file and was sure it was done right this time so she put it away and grabbed the next one.

It was late in the afternoon when Brandon poked his head into the office. "Grace," He said brightly.

Looking up, Grace had to try not to grimace at the sight of him. Instead, she said, "Yes?"

"Um, I was wondering if you'd like to go to the Festival of Lights with me next week?" He asked.

His tone, to Grace's way of thinking, sounded almost shy. Weird for a guy that seemed so wrapped up in himself and his apparent girl-catching ability.

She didn't know what to say, "I don't know, I didn't know anything about it," she answered.

"It's supposed to be pretty good, a fair-type of thing." Brandon stepped into the office.

Trying to get some control, Grace asked him, "Can I get back to you in a few days?"

Brandon nodded and wore a cocky smile, "Sure."

'Ahhh,' Grace thought, 'there was the Brandon she knew.'

He left her alone, thankfully. She'd have to refuse his offer but didn't have the energy to do it today.

After work, she went home and went up to her room. There were emails she needed to answer and she really had to start her paperwork for the new school semester.

Sitting at her desk, Grace just stared at her laptop.

After a few minutes, she jumped and startled herself. This behavior had to stop and stop now! She couldn't wander through her days and wonder about Tavin and that kiss and all the things she didn't say to him.

She went downstairs and into the kitchen to grab a phone book.

After searching through the white pages, she found his number and punched it into her phone.

Before she could chicken out, she hit the call button.

One ring, two rings, finally, she heard the line connect.

"Hello?" A voice answered.

Swallowing the lump of nerves that was sticking in her throat, Grace said, "Hello Tavin."

Tavin just got down off his horse when he heard his phone go off. He nodded thanks to his ranch hand who led the animal away.

As soon as the voice spoke, he knew who it was. "Grace," He said in response.

Smiling at the fact that he knew her voice, Grace took a breath, "I wanted to know if you were busy."

Tavin could hear her nerves, he had plenty of his own right now. "I'm not," He answered.

"Good," Grace said and wondered what she was going to say now. "Um, I was hoping we could talk."

Walking toward his house, he smiled. He was hoping they could talk about what happened. "Sure, do you want to drive out here or do you want to meet somewhere?" He asked.

Grace was starting to panic. She honestly didn't think he'd be too open to talk to her. Now what?

Her silence said a lot to Tavin. "My ranch is the next one down from Seth's, why don't you drive out and we'll go for a ride."

"Okay," Grace answered before she could think.

Tavin smiled, "Okay, I'll see you in a little bit then."

Hearing the line go dead, Grace stood in her aunt's kitchen and stared at nothing.

"Are you okay?" Melissa asked.

She watched her niece come into the room and make a phone call. She couldn't help but notice the slide-like display of emotions run across Grace's face. If was anyone else other than her niece, she might have gotten a kick out of it.

Once she put down her phone, Grace noticed her aunt. "I'm going to go out for a little bit," She announced and left the room.

Melissa waited for Grace to leave before she grabbed her cell phone and called Raelynn. She waited for her friend to answer before saying, "You'll never guess what just happened...."

It only took Grace fifteen minutes to get to Tavin's place. She recognized the sign for Seth's place and slowed down so she wouldn't miss the driveway leading to Tavin's house.

A few minutes later, she saw the mailbox that said, "McCormick," and turned down the lane.

It was a long driveway, much the same as the one leading to Seth's ranch. She thought that having the house set back probably provided some privacy for the residents.

Finally, she saw buildings and slowed down a little. Not that you could go fast, it was a gravel driveway with holes carved out here and there from weather.

The driveway had a fork, one way led to a circular drive in front of the main house and the other way led over to where the barns were. She saw someone standing in the window of the house so she followed the drive to the house.

Putting the car in park, Grace pulled a little mirror out of her purse and checked her appearance. She certainly looked better but this wasn't a date. It was talking.

She got out of the car and looked at the house. It was a farmhouse. She guessed it was old by the style, but it was well kept, the paint a bright white with green shutters around the windows. The porch seemed to wrap around it. There were even rocking chairs out front and Grace thought she was transported back to simpler times. It was lovely.

Tavin went out the front door to greet his guest and was surprised at how nervous he was. As soon as they hung up earlier, he jumped into the shower to clean off the grime from the day. After changing into clean jeans and shirt, he paced the floor in the entryway, waiting for her.

Grace walked up to the porch as Tavin reached the top step. They each stopped where they were and looked at one another.

Thoughts ran through Grace's mind but none of them seemed appropriate to say. She had questions too. Why did she come here? Even standing here, looking at Tavin, she couldn't answer the questions.

"Hello Grace," Tavin said and broke up the pile of thoughts accumulated in her mind.

"Hello Tavin," Grace said back.

Still, they both stood where they were. It was like they were each waiting for the other to blink.

Tavin stood there and watched her. She was beautiful. Her hair moved with the breeze, its wisps tickling her cheeks and making him wonder how the skin would feel against his fingertips.

Even for November, the temperature was mild. She was dressed in a long-sleeved tshirt, jeans, and boots. She was, for all intents and purposes, covered from head to toe and yet, he wanted her. The thought threw him emotionally.

"How are you?" He asked, then thought he sounded like a complete ass for asking.

Grace chuckled, "I'm fine Tavin." She took a breath, "But I'm figuring that you didn't ask me to come over to find that out." She climbed up the first step to the porch.

Tavin shook his head, "No, I sure didn't."

Climbing the next step, Grace felt a little more confident. "Why did you ask me over then?" The question came out smoothly, like a cat's purr.

It was easy to stand there and watch Grace get closer. The hard part was getting his body to calm down enough to be a gentleman. With each step, his body was responding more intensely.

She took another step up and asked, "No answer?"

"Uh," Tavin mumbled. He didn't know what the hell to say to her.

Grace stopped where she was, only two steps away from where Tavin stood, and just watched him. It was kind of comical how he looked tied up. 'Good,' Grace thought to herself, 'he deserved to be as confused as I am.'

Tavin cleared his throat, "Are you going to kiss me again then slap me?" He asked.

The question surprised Grace into laughing. "To be honest," She answered, "I am not sure."

Tavin nodded. At least she was honest. He wanted to kiss her so badly, his whole body ached. He wanted to feel her lips on his, wanted her to let him taste her for as long as he could.

"What did you think was going to happen if you came over here Grace?" Tavin asked in a low voice.

She reached the top step. He was only a foot away from her. She could reach out and touch him if she wanted to.

He stood there, in his jeans and t-shirt, and looked like he just stepped off the page of a magazine. His hair was slightly mussed and she could see it was wavy. If he let it grow out, it was probably curly.

Thinking of something so personal made her blush.

Grace looked up at him, her eyes meeting his for the first time. "I thought you would try to seduce me and I would be strong and not let you."

Her response was like setting a flame to kerosene. His body went into full alert; there was no mistaking the tone in her voice.

"Really?" He asked.

Nodding, Grace took the last step up so they were now on even ground. They should always be on even ground as far as she was concerned.

Tavin cocked his head to the side, "So you think that I only asked you over here to try and seduce you?"

Grace nodded again, "Most definitely."

Oh, this game they were playing was a dangerous one. Tavin wanted nothing more than to do just what she said but there was too much to work out between them. What Seth's friend, Melissa, said earlier plagued his conscience.

In a more serious tone, Tavin said, "Your aunt said I was cruel to you and I drove you away."

The words dowsed her desire in one full swoop. Instead of the arousal she felt only moments ago, Grace was embarrassed. How could Melissa tell him that?

"What?" Grace asked with hurt in her eyes.

Tavin knew he blew any chance of intimacy but it didn't matter right now. What mattered was that he was honest with Grace.

He talked with Seth and realized what he may have considered as a mere blip of a situation was a whole big mess of a situation where Grace was concerned. He hurt a young girl deeply and, if his mother were here, she'd tan his hide for doing it. Shame filled him for the last week and he knew he had to make amends in order for both of them to move on.

She did him a favor by calling and opening the door. Now he needed to be the one to close it again, only more gently.

It all seemed so easy in theory. That was, of course, until his eyes saw her in front of his house. She was certainly grown up now and other feelings tried to drown out his gentlemanly gestures.

"Your aunt," Tavin repeated, "she said that I hurt you and was cruel." He waited for the words to sink in and added, "And I knew I needed to apologize to you."

Anger, quick and sharp, filled Grace's mind. "You look at me the way you just did and expect me to think that you just wanted me to come over so you could say sorry?"

Her words cut his feelings. They were clipped and sharp, like razor blades.

Nodding, because words escaped him, Tavin stood there with his fists in his pockets.

"You're an ass!" Grace shouted. The volume surprised them both.

Tavin nodded again, "I know, I should never have said what I did to you at the drive in."

Grace looked at him, astonished at his words. "Have you lost your damned mind?" She looked around, hoping this was some weird joke. "You let me kiss you the way I did the other day and you think this is about what happened 4 years ago?"

Feeling a little lost, Tavin looked at her closely. She was riled up alright. Unfortunately, he knew they had to get past the first kiss. The second one, in his mind, was her just getting even and she did that in spades.

"Yes," He answered.

Without thinking, Grace slapped him. The "thwack" from the action cut through the evening air.

Grace regretted hitting him as soon as she did it but it was too late now. She couldn't speak so she turned and went back down the stairs to her car.

Chapter 9

Tavin stood on his porch and watched Grace drive back down his driveway. So much for wanting to do the right thing? He waited until he couldn't see her car lights before turning to walk inside. He rubbed his still sore, cheek while he did.

Grace pulled into her aunt's driveway and screeched to a halt.

"What the hell is wrong with him?" She yelled to no one.

Dropping her head so her forehead rested on the steering wheel, she let the first tears slip down her cheeks.

Never, in her whole life, had someone angered her so much that she slapped them. It seemed barbaric to stoop to the level. And yet, here she was, slapping Tavin McCormick across the face twice in one week.

Maybe he wasn't the stupid one here? Maybe it was her?

Nothing would be worked out now, she was sure of that.

Getting out of her car, she walked up to the door and glanced in the window before she opened the door. She caught a glimpse of Melissa and John walking into the kitchen. They were holding one another and laughing. The image was so sweet, Grace didn't want to interrupt their nice evening with her silly issues.

She turned and went for a walk.

A half hour later, Grace returned to her aunt's house and climbed up onto the porch. She heard raised voices from inside and opened the door, worried that something happened.

She stepped inside and said, "Aunt Melissa," loudly.

Stopping in her tracks, she saw Melissa with a finger pointed at Tavin and John looking really mad.

"Grace," Tavin said, "please explain to these two that I didn't lay a hand on you."

Looking at Tavin, Grace was confused. What was he doing here? What were the three of them doing?

Grace looked over at her aunt, "He didn't lay a hand on me." She said dryly.

Melissa frowned, she didn't know what to think. Tavin pounded on her front door a few minutes earlier, demanding to speak to Grace and she didn't even know Grace was home. They looked upstairs and, not finding her, started arguing about what happened at Tavin's ranch.

Diffusing the situation seemed like the best thing to do so Grace walked over and grabbed Tavin's arm.

She led him through the house and out onto the back porch. There was a swing there and she motioned for him to sit down.

Once he was seated, she turned around and asked, "What are you doing here?"

Tavin stood behind her, she had her back to him and he wanted to see her face, "I wanted to talk to you and we didn't do that while you were at my place."

'He made it sound so simple,' Grace thought to herself. 'Nothing was simple.'

When Grace didn't respond, Tavin spoke up, "When I kissed you 4 years ago, I was scared because I never wanted anyone so badly."

Grace turned around to face him, her eyes clouded with doubt.

Tavin bit his lip before he spoke again, "You see, I just wanted to be close to you and that kiss," he stopped and paced for a few steps, "the kiss made me want something I never did before."

She wanted to say something but couldn't. She nodded and let him know to continue.

"I'm ten years older than you Grace," He bit out the words like they were diseased. "You were only 17 and I was 27, I should have known better!"

Grace plopped down on the bench, "I thought I was just too inexperienced or something," she mumbled.

Hearing the hurt in Grace's voice tore at Tavin's heart. Seeing how much he hurt her was really wearing him down. He only knew their relationship wasn't right back then.

"No," He said and sat down beside her. "Even being that much older than you, I never kissed anyone like that before."

What did he mean? "I don't understand," Grace answered.

Tavin sighed, "I'm not even sure about it myself, Grace."

"So what now?" Grace asked.

Looking out into the darkness of the backyard, Tavin shook his head, "Damned if I know."

Grace laughed. It was either that or cry and she wasn't going to cry.

"I'm glad you find humor in my turmoil," Tavin said playfully.

Reaching over, Grace took his hand into hers. "One of the things you'll, no doubt, find charming about me."

'Oh she is a spitfire,' Tavin thought to himself. He looked over and into her eyes. They were reflecting the lights of the patio and shined brightly. How could he feel so conflicted about another person and just "want" so much at the same time.

"I'd like to kiss you," Tavin whispered as he leaned closer to Grace. "But I don't want to be slapped afterwards okay?"

A tear slipped down Grace's cheek, "Okay," she whispered back and leaned toward him.

Their lips met. And, just like before, chaos ensued. Grace's heart was beating strong and fast and her palms ached to touch Tavin. When she placed her hands on his shoulders and moved into his embrace, it was like all the insecurities inside her were being laid to rest in one moment.

The softness of his lips, mixed with the feel of his strength beneath her fingers, made her feel the most exquisite mix of craziness and sereneness all at the same time.

Tavin groaned and parted his lips to allow her to kiss him fully. When her tongue found his, the groan grew into a growl and he pulled her closer to him.

Their tongues were pirouetting around one another and making his body sing with excitement. His heart, he was pretty sure, was actually skipping beats because it was so excited.

Her nearness was intoxicating. He could smell the sweetness of her perfume mixed with her flowery shampoo. Reaching up, he touched her hair with his fingertips and was rewarded with their soft tickling on his nerve endings. It was exactly what he thought it would be like earlier when she got out of her car at his place.

Needing air, Grace pulled back and broke their connection. She laid her head against his shoulder and took a moment to regain her equilibrium.

"How can you think that wasn't mind blowing?" Tavin asked her.

Grace smiled, "I can't," she answered softly.

They sat there, Grace in his arms, on the swing and watched the stars come out from their daylight hiding places.

Hearing the crickets and the other night sounds, and in Tavin's arms, Grace thought it was about the loveliest spot in the world.

After a while of sitting there in silence, Grace asked, "I'm still not sure what you meant earlier about that kiss."

He knew what she meant and still struggled to find the right words.

"Grace," He shifted so he could face her. "I compete in rodeos."

She looked at him, "Okay?" She asked, "How does that affect a kiss?"

"In all my years of competing, I've met a lot of girls," He knew the words sounded awful, but he needed her to understand. "And I've kissed a few," He said sheepishly.

Grace's brow furrowed, "That's code for a lot right?" She asked.

Tavin nodded. "Yes," He sighed, "anyway, I never felt like I did when you kissed me by the lake."

She was torn between being flattered and appalled at his apparent "experience" with women. She nodded to encourage him to go on.

"I just had to kiss you." He whispered. "I should've known I shouldn't, I knew a lot of those kids you were with and knew their ages."

Sitting up, Grace started to understand, "Did you feel "wrong" about kissing me?" She asked.

He nodded again, "When Hailey said you were still in high school, all I could think of was that I was some sort of sick man."

Grace felt sorry for him. "Yes, I was still in high school Tavin but I was almost eighteen." She rubbed his arm, "It wasn't like you were trolling around the high school looking for underage girls."

The fact brought him a little relief from his guilt but he still felt like he was wrong in kissing her. And then wanting so much more from that one kiss just made him feel like some sick old man.

"I'm 22 now Tavin," Grace said softly, "do you still feel like kissing me is wrong?"

There was the big, fat problem in Tavin's mind. Having her be so much younger should make him feel bad but he sure as hell didn't.

Tavin looked into her eyes, "No, but," he started and her fingers on his lips stopped him.

Grace shook her head, "No buts, I'm an adult and I choose to be with you." She rubbed his hands absently with her own, "If I want to kiss you or make love with you, then I'll let you know."

The words 'make love' skittered through his gut and created a roaring response from his libido. Dear Lord, she was going to drive him mad.

"If I don't," Grace added, "then I'll let you know that too."

Why did she make it sound so simple? He didn't know but wanted to be sure like she seemed to be. Sure that this was all okay.

Tavin looked down at her and smiled, "I'm 32 years old, Grace." He stood up and started pacing again. "That's too old to be taking advantage of a young girl."

She wanted to laugh, but she held back. In his mind, the numbers didn't match up. Okay, she could live with that. But now, she needed to make him see that those numbers didn't mean anything.

"So," She looked up at him, "since you're so much OLDER than I am, we can't date?" She asked sarcastically.

Tavin sighed and answered, "We shouldn't."

Grace's last reserve of patience was used up by his words. "Are you kidding me?" She asked in astonishment.

He looked down and answered, "No."

"Why," Grace stood up and started pacing the length of the patio, "do all of our conversations end up with me thinking you're an ass?"

Tavin's shackles were coming up, "Now listen here," he started but shut up when he saw the murderous look in her eyes.

Grace stomped over to him and stuck a finger into his chest, "I can vote, I can drink, I can fire a weapon, which I might add, you should be happy I don't have in my possession right now," she took a breath, "but I'm too young to date a guy who's in his thirties." She dropped her hand and walked away, "Do you have any idea how ridiculous that sounds?"

'Well, when she put it that way,' Tavin thought to himself but didn't respond to her outburst.

Grace turned around to face him and shouted, "So you think I'm a virgin or something."

Now the conversation was getting a little more personal and Tavin felt the sting of embarrassment.

"I'm not, by the way," Grace said slowly, "I know how to please a man Tavin."

His head shot up and he glared at her.

Grace knew she struck a nerve, "I know how it feels to have a man's hands on my, touching me, feeling me, and I damned well know how to please him until he's all used up and exhausted."

If she wanted to see his anger, she just opened the door. "Grace," He spat out her name, "I would prefer it if you didn't speak that way."

"Great," Grace yelled, "now you're speaking to me like my father."

Tavin clenched his jaw, "Grace that's not fair," he said tightly.

Grace nodded in agreement, "You're right, Tavin, it's not fair." She started crying, "It's not fair that you kiss me and tell me that kissing me made you "feel" things no one ever had then tell me that I'm too young for you."

He understood what she meant, he was as confused as a bronc in a corral full of pretty fillies. He simply did not know what to do.

Trying to gain some composure, Grace swiped at the tears still on her cheeks. She sighed and said,

"There is no law that says I'm too young for you, so why are you hurting me?"

Damned if he knew. She was right.......about everything. He shook his head and shrugged, "I don't know," he answered.

"How can you not know?" Grace asked in amazement. "It's very simple to me Tavin, either you want to be with me or you don't."

Tavin walked over to her and took her in his arms, "I do," he said, desperation lacing his words.

Grace moved her head up so she could look into his eyes, "Then show me," she whispered.

Everything around them stood still. Tavin felt like the whole world was now moving in slow motion as he lowered his head. His lips anticipated the feel of hers and tingled with need. Once he touched her lips with his, all the doubts in his mind flew out the window her touch created.

His hands moved up and held her cheeks so he could focus on kissing her.

Grace opened her mouth to take him in and sighed when his tongue swirled around hers. 'Oh yes,' she thought, 'this is the kiss that every woman hopes she'll get.'

He was taking and she was giving, then she was taking and he was giving. The kiss was like the lightness of the breeze, as it moved across your skin or the amazement in seeing fireflies dot a deserted meadow on a summer evening, or like the first taste of ice cream, its coolness slipping across your taste buds. It was the excitement of a first with the knowledge that it wouldn't be the last. It was just……..everything.

Tavin pulled away first, sure that if he kept kissing her, he would lay her down in the grass and make love to her.

Grace's chest was heaving and she was so happy she wanted to run through the yard and yell "Yes!"

She laid her head against his chest and sighed.

"I don't know about you," Grace said into the fabric of his t-shirt, "but I really don't care about our age difference right now and I'm pretty sure you don't either at this point."

Smiling, Tavin hooked his finger under her chin and gently lifted it so she was looking up at him, "I will concede this point ma'am."

The combination of his accent with the words made Grace's smile widen.

"When will I see you again?" She asked.

Tavin's smile faded, "I don't know, I leave for a rodeo tomorrow and I'll be back next week," He answered in a flat tone.

"We're going riding at Seth and Raelynn's place tomorrow in the afternoon," Grace said.

Not knowing what to say, Tavin added, "I'm sure you'll have a great time."

Grace nodded, "It would be better if you were going to be there."

She was saying what he was thinking. "I know darlin, it sure would be," he said.

Not wanting to leave her, but knowing he should, Tavin started moving toward the house.

Grace opened the door and they walked into the dining room. Melissa and John were nowhere to be found so Grace walked Tavin out to his truck and said goodbye.

Standing in her aunt's driveway, Grace wondered how they managed to get into all of this.

Chapter 10

The next afternoon, Melissa and Grace were getting ready for their ride when Raelynn came out to the barn to talk to them.

"I heard a rumor," Raelynn said slowly to Grace.

Looking annoyed, but not really being annoyed, Grace asked, "Yes?"

Raelynn puckered her lips as if she was in deep concentration, "I heard that a certain cowboy was over at my very best friend's house last night and kissing her niece out on the patio."

Blushing, Grace tried not to smile. "Is that so?" She asked while looking over at her aunt.

"Rumors start," Melissa said, trying to sound innocent.

Raelynn watched Melissa get up into the saddle, "Well?" She asked Grace.

Trying to use a southern accent, Grace said slowly, "I can report that a certain young man did show me some attention on the veranda of my aunt's home last night," she took a breath, "and I can report that the same young man did, indeed, kiss me until I was simply breathless." She batted her eyelashes and fanned herself with her hands to complete the look.

Laughing, Raelynn shook her head. "Sounds about right to me," she shot back at Grace.

Once Grace was up in the saddle, the two women led the horses out of the main ranch area just as they did the week before.

A few minutes into the ride, they spotted a rider coming toward them. It was weird because Seth's ranch was behind them.

Grace squinted to see if she knew who the rider was. Her mouth grew into a huge smile when she recognized him as Tavin.

"I'll be," Melissa whispered as she recognized the rider coming toward them. She looked over at her niece and said, "I think I'll head back and see John for a little while."

Grace sat where she was and watched her aunt turn around to go back to the ranch. When she turned back around, Tavin was getting closer and her heart beat was speeding up.

"What are you doing here?" Grace asked when he was close enough.

Tavin saw her riding and he knew she was meant to be on a horse. Her movements were sure and it was obvious how much she loved the animals. It kind of threw him since most of the women he met didn't like horses even though they seemed to really like the guys who rode them.

He pulled his horse up to stop and pushed his hat back a little so she could see his face, "I wanted to ride with you today before I left," he said.

Grace thought the gesture was so kind that she had to hold back tears. "You did?" She asked, in total surprise.

Nodding, Tavin turned his mount around so they were going in the same direction. "I did."

"Okay," Grace answered with a laugh.

They started out walking the horses but soon nudged the animals into full blown cantor.

Grace could see the trees passing by quickly, the wind was pushing at her hat but it was so tightly fitted on her head that it wouldn't budge. She suspected that Tavin's horse could easily leave Cindy in the dust but he kept his pace with hers.

After a few minutes, they came up to a clearing and there was a fence at the far side of it. Grace pulled up and stopped Cindy.

She looked at Tavin and asked, "Where to now?"

Smiling over at Grace, Tavin nodded toward the fence line. "Follow me," He said and started walking toward a small grove of trees.

Once they were close to the trees, Grace could make out a gate on the other side of them. "Ahh," She said.

"Don't worry," Tavin said, "we're going onto my land now."

Curious, Grace followed him and watched as he unhooked the latch on the gate. He backed up his horse to let Grace walk through first with Cindy, then rode through on his mount and re-latched the gate.

"Very handy," Grace said.

Tavin nodded. He guided his horse away from the fence and Grace followed.

They walked for a while, enjoying the scenery. The space was wide open, as if they were the only people in the whole world. There were groups of trees dotting the landscape and providing some shade to the cattle as they grazed.

"Is your ranch as big as Seth's?" Grace asked and then felt stupid for asking such a question.

Tavin looked over and smiled, "Mine's a little bigger, he would probably debate it, but the truth is, it is."

Grace laughed at his mischievous look. "I'll bet," She said playfully.

They walked for a little while longer, letting the horses take them wherever.

He watched her, the way she moved in the saddle, the way she would reach forward now and again to scratch her horse's ears, the way she would laugh when the horse whinnied a response. Watching her was like watching a new colt come into the world or watching the tall grass of a pasture sway in the breeze; it was just beautiful.

"You know you're beautiful right?" Tavin asked her as they rode along.

The question was so surprising that Grace couldn't answer right away. She finally said, "Thank you," and added, "No, I didn't since I don't see myself that way."

Tavin shook his head in exasperation, "Well, you are."

It was like he was just laying down the law or something. It was adorable and humbling at the same time. Grace smiled.

A few minutes later Tavin asked, "Would you like to actually see my ranch and my house?"

'Loaded question,' Grace thought. "Yes," She answered, "I'd love to."

Tavin nudged his horse and they took off. Grace and Cindy in hot pursuit behind them.

The horses ran until the buildings were in sight, then both Tavin and Grace slowed them down.

A couple of hands came out of the main barn when they rode up.

"Grace, this is my foreman, Rich, and one of our hands, Timmy," Tavin said.

Nodding to the men, Grace said, "Hello."

Tavin jumped down, "Guys, this is Ms. Harris," he said as he handed the reins to Rich.

Grace shook her head and said, "Oh please just call me Grace."

Rich nodded, "Greetings, Ms. Grace," he responded.

Timmy echoed, "Ms. Grace," and tipped the end of his hat to her.

Tavin helped her down and smiled as she slid down into his arms.

The men sure made her feel.......delicate. That's the only word she could come up with. It was sweet.

The men took the horses away and Tavin took Grace's hand into his. They took a tour of the barn, Grace asking questions here and there about things that she found interesting.

Tavin pointed out a few other buildings and told her what they were used for.

Finally, they ended up at the house.

Grace had to admit, she wondered about where Tavin lived.

They walked inside and Grace's breath hitched in her chest.

The house was gorgeous! They walked into a great room done up in light wood. The beams in the ceiling were stained a darker color to show contrast and it made the room look even larger.

Tavin took her through the main floor, pointing out the dining room and kitchen. He told her there was a den downstairs as well as a half bath. He excused himself when the phone rang and left Grace to her own devices.

She remembered seeing pictures on the wall in the living room so she went back in there. The far wall was covered with photographs.

Some were recent ones of Tavin but some were very old. She walked along the wall slowly, looking at each image closely. One of the pictures had a date on it of 1905 on the bottom of it. The two people in it were looking at the camera but not smiling. Grace supposed they weren't sure what was going on.

"I couldn't take them down," Tavin said from behind Grace. He came back to find her looking at his family pictures in the great room.

Grace was puzzled, "Why would you?" She smiled at him, "Take them down?"

Tavin looked at the wall, "Because they've been there forever and I redid the house, but I just couldn't leave them off."

'How silly,' Grace thought, 'that he thought he had to take them down.'

"I think they're perfect," Grace sighed.

He stood behind her silently while she moved slowly. She wanted to see every picture and took her time. She pointed to a few and he patiently explained who was in it.

When Grace got to the last picture, she laughed. It was of a, what she assumed, very young Tavin in a diaper with chaps and boots on.

"Yes," He answered her unspoken question, "that's me."

Grace smiled big, "You were so cute!"

Tavin said in mock horror, "Was?"

Giving him a look of "Whatever," Grace traced the shape of him on the picture.

Finally, she stepped away from the wall and noticed his bags were in the entryway.

"For your trip?" She asked as she nodded toward the bags.

Tavin nodded, "We were supposed to leave this morning but I told the guys to go ahead and get the animals set up, I'll leave later."

Touched again, that he would wait to leave so he could go riding with her, Grace leaned over and kissed his cheek.

Just a peck on the cheek from Grace made his body go into hyper drive. He blushed at the direction his thoughts went.

Grace walked away from him and stood in the middle of the room, "Where is your bedroom?" She asked.

"Oh no," Tavin said and walked up to her to take her in his arms, "if I show you my room, I won't go to the rodeo I've paid a small fortune to enter into."

Testing her power over him, Grace nipped his lower lip with her teeth. "Oh, I was hoping you could show me your bed."

Her tone was slowly driving him insane, "I'll just bet you want to see my bed," he said teasingly.

"I do," Grace smiled and wiggled her eyebrows. "Of course, I'd want to test it out a little too," The words were drawn out.

Knowing he was playing with fire, Tavin turned her around so she was facing away from him and he marched her out through the kitchen. It was bad enough the next week would be filled with him wondering about her and his bed, he didn't want to make it any worse.

They were outside and Tavin walked her back over to the barn.

The guys brought their horses back out and Tavin helped Grace get up into the saddle. She watched him in fascination as he effortlessly jumped up into his own saddle.

They rode back to Seth's ranch slowly. They talked about the rodeo Tavin was riding in and Grace asked a lot of questions. She wasn't familiar with rodeos and what was involved.

Tavin patiently told her about the events he preferred, Bronc riding and team roping. He used to ride bulls but said it was a 'young man's game' now. Grace got impatient with his self-deprecating tone where his age was concerned. It wasn't like he was 60! She made a mental note to say something when he returned from his trip.

When the ranch buildings were close, Tavin pulled up his horse. "I've got to turn around and head home so I can hit the road," He nodded to Seth's place, "Are you okay for the rest of the way?"

Grace appreciated his concern, even if it was misplaced, "Yes," she answered. "Please be safe," She said.

Tipping his hat to her, Tavin smiled, "Oh yes ma'am," he answered and took off.

Grace watched him go with a mixture of sadness and awe.

When she entered the main area of Seth's ranch, she saw John and Melissa come out of the barn to greet her.

"Hey there," Melissa said and asked, "how was your ride?"

Grace smiled, "Very nice, thank you."

John helped her down from the saddle and Grace couldn't help but wish it were Tavin instead.

Melissa took her arm, "He'll be back soon," she whispered, knowing the look on her niece's face.

Nodding, Grace knew her aunt was right, but it still didn't stop her from missing Tavin already.

Chapter 11

The next few days consisted of Grace getting up, going to work with her aunt, and coming home to think about Tavin.

Sitting on her bed, she wondered what it was about him that drew her in so deeply.

He was tall with wide shoulders. His face was nice but not classically handsome. His hair was thick but pretty unruly, especially since he wore a cowboy hat. The natural curl tried to take over as soon as he removed it.

During their kisses, she really only felt his arms and shoulders, but she could imagine how the rest of him felt.

The road her thoughts were taking was becoming emotionally treacherous so Grace decided it was best to focus on other things. Thanksgiving was coming up in a little over a week and she had yet to get a gift list together.

Getting on her computer, Grace scanned her emails and answered a couple from college friends. People were acting so surprised when she mentioned that she was in Texas working.

She was getting ready to start her online search for Christmas gift ideas when she heard her aunt.

"Grace," Melissa called upstairs, "come down, Tavin is on TV."

Grace jumped up and ran downstairs. Not surprisingly, John was seated on the couch and stood when she entered the room.

She waved and sat down on the over-stuffed chair.

Sure enough, there was Tavin, riding a very agitated looking horse.

Her gaze glued to the television, Grace started to feel a mixture of horror and fear build up inside her. Why the hell would anyone do this?

Tavin was on the horse as it bucked and jumped and was determined to get him off of its back.

Watching the two of them was like watching a pair of dancers, trying to move together but apart at the same time.

A buzzer sounded and Tavin jumped off of the horse, landing on his hands and knees.

Grace's hand flew to her mouth, she was afraid he was hurt.

When he jumped up and dusted himself off, she sighed in relief.

As in any competition, there was a replay of his ride and then scores were shown on the screen. Grace had no idea if they were good or not and didn't care. Her focus was on Tavin and him being okay.

A commercial came on and Grace looked over at John and Melissa. They looked completely unfazed by what was happening on TV.

Grace couldn't help it, she blurted out, "Why would he do that?"

Melissa looked at her niece and saw that her complexion was white, as if she'd just been scared out of her mind. Rodeos were a common occurrence down here so it didn't even register with Melissa that Grace would be so upset by Tavin's participation.

John spoke up, "TJ's family has been in the rodeo for at least 3 generations. His daddy did it and his granddaddy did it too. He's really good."

Hearing the explanation didn't do any good in alleviating Grace's fears.

"I'm going back up to my room to do some online shopping," Grace said and got up to leave.

John stood up again and sat back down once she was out of the room. He looked at Melissa and frowned, "She didn't seem too well set on seeing TJ ride."

Melissa nodded, "Watching it is a little scary," she answered, "but I've been to rodeos so I don't think about it as much. I don't think she's ever been to one."

"It's a good thing the season is over for TJ then," John stated.

Melissa smiled and kissed him, "Yes, it is."

Grace was upstairs an hour later and didn't even see what was on the computer screen in front of her. She tried desperately to think of something else besides Tavin on that horse.

Her phone rang a few hours later, jostling Grace from her trance.

"Hello," She answered.

Tavin smiled when she answered, he wasn't sure she would, "Hello Grace," he said slowly.

Something about the way he said her name made her body tense in a completely different way. She smiled because she couldn't help herself.

"Tavin," She said on a sigh, and asked, "Are you alright?"

He could hear the concern in her voice, "Yes perty lady I am," he said using an amplified accent. "Why, are you okay?" Suddenly he was worried that something was going on with her.

Grace closed her bedroom door and plopped down on her bed before saying, "I saw you on TV and it was scary."

Tavin never really considered what he did scary. Rodeo was tough mentally and physically, but his family did it without much thinking. It was in their blood. Of course, he was getting to an age when he had to let go of it, but not just yet. Hearing Grace's worried tone had an odd effect on him, it made him happy for some reason.

"I'm just fine Grace," He said softly.

Grace sighed, "Good."

Not wanting to dwell on things that made her worry, Tavin changed the subject. "We're wrapping up here and I'll be home tomorrow." He waved absently to another cowboy who called out his name while passing and waited for Grace to respond.

Smiling now, Grace was happy. "Well, I suppose we'll have to go out on a date or something then won't we?" She asked in a sassy tone.

"That is exactly what I was thinking." Tavin answered. "Is it okay if I call you when we get back tomorrow?" He asked.

Anticipation started twirling around her insides like a tornado. All of her senses were swept up into the thought of seeing him again.

She laughed and said, "Yes!" In an animated voice.

Tavin laughed. Pleasing her seemed too easy if all it took was him coming home.

"I'll call you tomorrow," He said and added, "it will be later in the day."

"Okay," Grace answered. "Bye," She said and ended the call.

She sat on her bed for a long time and thought about how unconcerned Tavin sounded when he talked about being in the rodeo.

Maybe it wasn't as bad as she thought. Thinking that understanding something is the key to curing fear, Grace got up and went to her computer. She googled "rodeo injuries" and almost fainted with the amount of articles that came up.

Scanning them, Grace became more concerned. "Holy crap," She said out loud when a particularly graphic picture popped up on the screen of a bronc rider in, what appeared to be, excruciating pain.

There were pictures of cowboys being caught up in stirrups and being dragged by bulls or horses.

Looking at the articles and pictures only intensified her fears instead of alleviating them.

After hours of reading articles and looking at gruesome pictures, Grace's nerves were shot. She needed to get out of the house and away from this.

She went downstairs and called out to her aunt, "I'm going out for a little while."

Melissa stuck her head around the corner of the doorway leading to the kitchen, "Okay, have fun," she answered.

Grace nodded and opened the door. She got into her car and didn't really know where to go. Driving around aimlessly didn't really appeal to her so she decided to go over to the local mall.

Even though it wasn't Thanksgiving yet, the parking lot was still pretty full. Finding a parking spot close was not possible so she settled for the first one she came across and walked into the main entrance.

Christmas decorations were up and you could feel the upbeat mood. Grace smiled despite herself. She started walking down the main part of the mall, peeking in here and there if something in the display window caught her eye.

Grace ended up purchasing a few things; a brightly printed scarf she thought Melissa would love, a baby blanket for Raelynn and Seth's baby, a simple gold bracelet she thought her mother would like, and a box of Christmas cards she wanted to send to her friends. There was a goofy snowman on the front that made her laugh.

It was getting dark when she got back home. There was a note on the kitchen table from her aunt saying she and John went over to Seth and Raelynn's for dinner. There were leftovers in the refrigerator.

The thought of eating alone didn't appeal to Grace at all so she went back out and went to a movie. Maybe the distraction of someone else's problems would make hers seem less important.

She picked a comedy and sat down with her popcorn and hot dog. Before she was comfortably seated, she saw someone beside her. Turning around, she was going to smile politely until she saw who was next to her. It was Brandon from work. 'Oh great,' she thought, 'just what I need right now.'

Brandon smiled brightly, "Fancy meeting you here," he said in a smooth voice.

Just hearing the innuendo in his tone made the hair on Grace's neck stand up. She smiled tightly and sat down.

Luckily the lights dimmed and the previews started so Grace didn't feel like she was obligated to talk to him.

The movie was probably funny but Grace couldn't get into it. Between the thoughts of Tavin being crushed by an animal and Brandon's thinly veiled attempts to touch her hand on the arm rest between them, she was at her wits end when the lights of the theater came back up.

"I'll see you at work Monday," Grace said hurriedly as she scooted down the aisle toward the exit.

Grace was outside the theater and almost to her car when Brandon caught up to her. She heard him call after her but pretended not to hear him.

Brandon ran around her in the parking lot to get her attention, "Grace, didn't you hear me calling you?" He asked.

The tight smile back in place, Grace shook her head and said, "No, I'm sorry I didn't."

Lying was not something she particularly appreciated doing, but she really didn't want to have trouble at work.

"How about dinner?" Brandon asked her.

'No way!' Grace shouted inside her head. "I'm sorry," She said instead, "I can't tonight."

Brandon, not dissuaded by her refusal, asked, "Tomorrow then?"

It appeared that there was no good way of getting this guy to back down. She wanted to be diplomatic but he was making it hard.

"Listen Brandon," She said and lightly touched his arm, "I don't date people I work with and, besides that, I'm dating someone else right now." She was stern but nice with her tone.

Looking only slightly put off, Brandon took in the words then responded, "Well, I'm only there until the semester ends next month so I'll ask you again then."

Nodding, Grace didn't say anything else. She didn't want to encourage him. Instead, she just said, "Goodnight." And got into her car.

She wasn't completely comfortable until she was locked up inside her aunt's house. Every encounter with Brandon was an exercise in control. He unnerved her and she wasn't used to feeling that way. It was certainly unlike the feelings that Tavin evoked from her.

Her mind jumped to thoughts of her cowboy and his career. Why would he do that? Seeing how dangerous it is would have made her say, 'No Thank You.'

After a shower and a handful of peanuts as a snack, Grace was tucked into bed when she heard the front door open.

A minute later, Melissa's face popped into the doorway to her room, "How was your night," she asked Grace.

Grace sighed, "It was fine, yours?" She asked in return.

Melissa walked into the room and sat on the edge of the bed. "Well, it was great having dinner with Raelynn and Seth but seeing Raelynn so uncomfortable with the pregnancy worries me."

Nodding, Grace could understand concern for friends, "No offense," she started, "but she's in her 40's and that's high risk right?"

"None taken," Melissa answered, "and yes it is."

Putting the book she was reading aside, Grace leaned forward, and offered "If you'd like me to go out there to check on her, I'd be happy to do it."

"Yeah," Melissa answered, "that would also give you a convenient excuse to see Mr. TJ McCormick," she raised her eyebrows, daring Grace to deny it.

Grace tilted her head, "Maybe," she smiled. "But it wouldn't hurt for us to keep a close eye on her," she said in a serious tone.

Nodding, Melissa patted her niece's leg, "You are right about that." She stood up, "We'll work something out tomorrow."

"Okay," Grace answered, "Good night."

The responding, "Good night," was hollered down the hallway.

Chapter 12

Sunday morning proved to be bright and sunny, which matched Grace's mood. She was excited that she would see Tavin today.

The fears about his being in rodeos hadn't dissipated but she was determined to understand it in order to be closer to him.

Her brother called her after Melissa went to bed and they talked for over an hour. He wheedled information out of her better than any CIA operative. He got her to admit that she was seeing someone and even persuaded her to tell him about what happened the first time she met Tavin four years ago.

The phone call was actually therapeutic in that she heard herself say what she kept inside for far too long.

Since Brad was such a great big brother, he did say a few derogatory comments about Tavin's treatment of his sister, which made Grace love him more. After she explained it all, he told her he'd give this guy, Tavin, a chance.

Grace smiled when they hung up and was able to drift off into a peaceful dream full of cowboys and daisies.

After she got showered and dressed, Grace went downstairs to see what Melissa was up to.

Her aunt was at the stove making, what seemed to be, pancakes.

Melissa turned around at the sound of Grace coming down the hallway into the kitchen. "Good morning," She said to her niece as she flipped the pancake on the griddle.

"What are you making?" Grace asked.

Smiling, Melissa said, "Pancakes, in the shape of the great state of Texas," and flipped the misshapen flapjack onto a plate.

Rolling her eyes, Grace took the plate and smiled benignly. If her aunt wanted to make weird looking pancakes, it was her prerogative.

Melissa sat down next to Grace at the table and sliced off a tab of butter from the dish. "So, what's on your agenda for today?" She asked Grace.

Grace was done with the butter part and moved on to soaking her pancake with copious amounts of syrup. The first bite was awesome!

After enjoying their breakfast, Melissa went in her room to change while Grace cleaned up. That was the deal, whoever cooked didn't clean.

"You never answered my question," Melissa said when she came out from getting ready, "What's on the agenda today?"

Putting the plates away, Grace said over her shoulder, "I'm supposed to see Tavin sometime later today, and I'm going to pass the rest of the day trying to figure out Christmas gift ideas."

"Sounds like fun," Melissa said slyly.

Grace shot her a look that said, 'PUHLEEEZ.'

They finished clearing up the mess from breakfast and Grace went up to get her laptop from her room. She perched herself at the kitchen table, a pad of paper and pen on one side and a cup of hot cocoa on the other.

Melissa came in a few minutes later to say she was going to a mall in Houston with John to start their Christmas shopping.

"Good luck," Grace shouted after her aunt.

The house was quiet but that didn't bother Grace. She was focused on the task at hand and was glad when she found a rare book she knew her mother would enjoy and a very beautiful blazer for her dad.

She was still at it when lunchtime rolled around so she made herself a quick sandwich and stayed logged in trying to find unique gifts.

It was sometime later when her phone rang. She looked at the caller ID and saw it was Tavin.

"Hello there, are you home?" She asked.

Tavin smiled, just hearing her voice made him do that. He hated that she was probably waiting for him.

"We hit something and did some damage to the front of my truck," He said while waving to one of his hands to move their truck around. "I'm stuck here until it's fixed."

The let down from his news was big. Grace couldn't quite hide it from her voice. "It's okay, Tavin." She said quietly.

He knew it wasn't but he was grateful that she was letting it go. He'd dated women much older than she was who pitched fits if things didn't go exactly as they planned.

One of his guys was motioning for him to come over to where the mechanic was looking at the truck so Tavin put up one finger to say, 'One Minute.'

"I appreciate you not giving me grief about this, it doesn't make me happy. I wanted to see you tonight." He said, impatience making his voice tight.

'He's such a worrier,' Grace thought to herself. "I'm fine, thanks for calling me," She said.

After she hung up, Grace felt let down. The day seemed to loom in front of her like a big empty box.

A couple of hours later, Melissa and John came in the front door, loaded down with boxes. When Melissa came into the kitchen and saw the look on Grace's face, she figured something was up.

"I see you're still here," Melissa said softly.

Grace did not like the look of pity her aunt was giving her. She was an adult and certainly didn't need a man to give her purpose.

Standing up, Grace went over to the coffee pot and poured some more water into her cup of hot cocoa.

She looked at her aunt and smiled, "It's fine auntie; he was just delayed."

Looking at her aunt, Grace realized that her aunt didn't believe her. The pity was the worst part.

John came in and sat down at the table. He smiled at the women, hoping there was a promise of dinner in the near future.

"How about we grill out something?" Melissa asked.

Grace nodded, "Sounds good, I'll get the salad together."

Without saying anything else, the three of them got to work and made dinner quickly. It was nice, having the company and Grace found herself relaxing as they set the table.

The dinner conversation was light. They discussed the chaotic mall environment and John relayed his shopping horror stories as he saw them.

Grace laughed at the dramatic inflections he used. It was completely unlike his day to day personality.

Melissa threw in a few hints about her Christmas wishes and Grace laughed at the way John pretended not to hear her.

After dinner, Grace cleaned up, refusing offers from Melissa and John to help, and went up to her room.

The quiet of the night should be soothing but she found herself thinking about Tavin and wishing she would have been able to see him.

When she finally fell asleep, hours later, she was riddled with dreams of Tavin and the kisses they shared.

Monday morning was sunny but Grace's mood wasn't.

Her subconscious never seemed to settle down so when the alarm went off, it felt like she hadn't slept at all.

Even Melissa was quiet while they ate breakfast and got their bags together to go into the office.

Grace didn't hang around the break room, she went into Raelynn's office and dug in straight away. Work was the only rational thing she could do right now.

All the doubts and fears about Tavin and their tumultuous past were just at the surface and she couldn't seem to settle them.

The morning flew by and she was feeling better by lunchtime. Melissa had lunch brought in for the four of them so everyone sat down together.

Amy sat there quietly and ate delicate little bites of the salad and pasta.

Brandon talked with Melissa about a client's demands, while Grace listened intently.

The time with Brandon was pleasant for a change so Grace thought maybe the guy got her message of "back off" loud and clear.

When they went back to work, Grace was feeling much more focused and content.

At about 4 o'clock, Grace was doing some filing when she looked up to find Brandon in the doorway. He had a smug look on his face and that made Grace feel very uncomfortable.

"Brandon," Grace said coolly, "did you need something?"

Grace watched, with a decided amount of dread, as he walked into the office and stood just a couple of feet in front of her.

Brandon smiled, "I really enjoyed seeing the movie with you the other day," he said smoothly.

Grace's gut tightened with nervousness. The tone of his voice set her on edge.

"Listen," She started to say, but he interrupted her.

Brandon lifted a hand and put it on Grace's shoulder, he loved the way she smelled.

He touched a loose tendril of her hair and said, "I can't wait for our next date."

Grace was just about to tell him to back off when she heard a noise. She looked over Brandon's shoulder into the eyes of a very annoyed looking Tavin.

"Am I interrupting something?" Tavin asked in an overly calm voice.

He felt so bad about cancelling on Grace that he wanted to surprise her with some flowers. Raelynn told him where to go so he was all smiles when he got to the office. That was, until he saw some young punk telling Grace how great of a time they had the other night. It didn't sit well with him.

Brandon's shoulders came up as if he were trying to make himself seem taller.

Grace wanted to laugh at the obvious display of testosterone but, seeing the look on Tavin's face, she decided it wasn't the time for that.

"No," She rushed, "Brandon was just leaving."

It was clear that Brandon didn't know he was leaving since he shot Tavin a nasty look.

Grace watched as Brandon slowly moved around Tavin and then turned when he was in the doorway and said, "I'll see you soon."

Tavin wanted to punch the jackass in the face but he was smart enough to know better. He spent too many years being a hot head and getting into trouble. Age gave him wisdom but it didn't stop him from wanting to teach this Brandon kid a lesson.

After Brandon left, Grace sighed in relief. The kid was going to be more of a problem than she first thought. She looked up and got the first good look of Tavin as he stood, looking a little uncomfortable, in her office.

"Are those for me?" Grace asked, nodding at the flowers.

Tavin snapped back to the present. "Uh yes," He answered and walked over to her.

Taking the flowers, Grace held them up to her nose and inhaled the beautiful scents. They were a lovely mix of wild flowers.

She looked at Tavin and said, "Thank you, they're beautiful."

Still thinking about Grace with that other guy, Tavin just nodded and stood there.

'Okay,' Grace thought, 'this is awkward.' She knew he was still ticked off about what he thought he saw with her and Brandon. Normally, she would've explained herself but she was feeling particularly surly and didn't offer up anything.

Tavin stood there and looked at Grace holding the bouquet. She was beautiful and he was right on in picking the mix of different flowers. They reminded him of her, being made up of different colors and scents. In the short amount of time he spent with Grace, she showed different sides of herself. He wanted to see more but if she was dating another guy, he wouldn't play that game.

"Are you dating him?" He finally asked. It was a risky question but he learned a long time ago that he didn't play with his feelings.

Grace turned to put the flowers on the credenza. She boosted herself up while looking away. "No," She said while still playing with the petals of a daisy. "He would like to date and I am not interested."

She finally turned around and looked as serious as her words were.

Tavin wanted to believe her. In the few times they were together, she always seemed so straightforward. That was a big part of his attraction. What did they do now?

Finally, Tavin nodded, "Okay," he said, then smiled, "would you like to go out to dinner with me then?"

The question threw Grace. One minute he looked really pissed off and then the next, he asks her out. 'Does it matter?' She asked herself. 'You want to spend time with him and this is your chance!'

Grace nodded yes, "I'll put these in a vase," she said and moved around him.

When Grace was out of the office, Tavin took a deep breath. He could smell the sweet scent of her perfume mixed with the aroma of the flowers.

She came back into the office and walked up to Tavin. Putting her hands around his neck, she looked up into his blue-green eyes and smiled. This is what she wanted, to be near him.

Leaning up, Grace kissed him softly on the lips.

The kiss, like everything else regarding Grace, was a mixture of soft and hard, sweet and intense. It took every ounce of willpower Tavin had to refrain from slamming the office door shut and taking her right there on the floor. Knowing that Melissa was in the next office, and was a good friend of Seth's, made him reluctantly pull back.

"Can we go now?" He asked through clenched teeth.

Grace was into the kiss and then he stopped. Feeling a little off balance, she was going to say something but looked into his eyes and saw something she couldn't describe. He almost looked mad. 'Did he not like the kiss?' She wondered.

Nodding, Grace stepped back and went around the desk to straighten up the pile of files and put her things away.

Ten minutes later, they were in Tavin's truck and driving down the road.

Realizing they were leaving Lake Jackson, Grace turned to Tavin and asked, "Can I ask where we're going?"

"No," He said and kept his eyes on the road.

Chapter 13

That was not the answer Grace was expecting and it put a very sharp edge on the anger building up inside her.

She sat on the passenger side and was very quiet for the rest of the trip. When they turned onto FM 1462 off of Hwy 288, she assumed they were going to his house. 'Well, why didn't he just say so?' She asked herself.

A few minutes later, Tavin pulled into the driveway of his ranch and drove faster than he normally would. He knew he answered her question the wrong way and now she was mad. He was really going to have to work on damage control if he wanted turn this date around.

When Tavin stopped the truck in front of his house, he shut off the engine and looked over at Grace.

"I'm sorry," He said, "I was being a smart ass and was still feeling raw about seeing you with that Brandon guy."

'At least he was honest,' Grace thought.

When she didn't answer, Tavin started getting nervous, "I wanted to bring you here," he unclipped his seatbelt, "and cook for you."

His tone was starting to sway her. Oh, she wanted to stay mad but the thought of him cooking was interesting.

"Okay," She answered and got out of the truck.

Tavin hurried up to jump out and come around the vehicle, "I was going to open your door for you," he said softly.

Still feeling annoyed, Grace smiled benignly, "Well, I figured I'd get it myself since you are "raw," I didn't think you'd want to help me out."

The words were sharp and hit their target. "I'm sorry," Tavin said.

Grace nodded, "I'm sorry too," she took the hand he offered her, "and I'm being a jerk."

They both apparently had some issues to work through.

"Why don't we start over," Tavin said and turned to face her. "I'd like you to join me for dinner now and I want you to feel comfortable in my home."

His words traveled over her skin just as a stone would skip over water. They made her feel little trickles of awareness inside. Grace loved the feeling. She only remembered having it with Tavin.

"Okay," She answered and touched the side of his face with the palm of her hand.

Feeling more settled, Tavin turned back toward the house and led her up the stairs. He opened the front door and waited for her to go in before following.

Grace stepped inside and her breath caught. She could see the great room in front of them and it was lit with candles. Not just one or two, but dozens of them all around. The glow from the flames danced on the walls and made the huge room seem intimate.

"It's lovely," Grace sighed.

Tavin smiled. Her reaction was what he hoped for. His foreman, and friend, Rich, told him that the candles were a good idea. Not that Tavin blabbed about his love life, but he did mention that he disappointed Grace the evening before. Being a married man for over 20 years, Rich knew a thing or two about women and made suggestions.

He took her hand and led her into the center of the room, where a fire blazed in the fireplace. He reached over and pulled a bottle of wine out of a bucket.

"Wine?" He asked.

Grace nodded, "Yes, that's lovely," she responded and noted the label of the wine was a very good one.

Tavin gestured toward a plush blanket spread out on the floor in front of the fire, "Why don't you sit here and enjoy your wine while I go and finish dinner."

Sitting down, she wondered if she should help. It felt…..wrong not to offer. "Can I give you a hand?" She asked.

Shaking his head no, Tavin smiled, "No thank you, I've got it. You just stay here and enjoy your wine."

"Okay," Grace answered.

She watched him walk out of the room and thought the whole thing was very odd. Him coming to her work, getting upset about Brandon, bringing her here; the whole thing threw her feelings into a tailspin of sorts.

Sitting back against the ottoman, Grace pulled her feet under her and studied the fire while she waited. The curtains in the room were closed so the only light was from the fire and the candles. She smiled when she heard the music start. 'Oh, he was thinking of everything,' she thought.

A few minutes later, Tavin came into the living room. He put down a tray on the ottoman and knelt down on the floor beside her.

"I cut up some vegetables for us to munch on while dinner is finishing," Tavin said.

The whole thing was just a little weird. Grace had to say something, "I would've never pegged you for a candle and romantic mood thing," she said.

Appreciating her honesty, Tavin blushed. "I'm not normally," he started, "but with you it felt right."

If that was his way of being honest, Grace loved it. "Really?" She asked.

Tavin nodded, "Yes," he picked up a baby carrot, dipped it in the ranch dressing, and popped it into his mouth. After he swallowed the bite, he said, "I see you in this whole romantic setting with gauzy white sheets, a breeze blowing through, you smiling."

Grace was pretty sure there was more to it than he described but he knew how to set the scene. "It sounds lovely," She responded.

Reaching over, Tavin ran the back of his fingers down her cheek. His breath hitched when she turned her head into his fingers and kissed them. The sensations were quick and the intensity of them took him by surprise.

"Tell me more," Grace whispered.

His fingers were strong and she kissed them as they ran down her cheek. The contact was very intimate and still kind of innocent. Grace's insides were screaming at her to touch him but she wanted to take it slowly.

Just watching her lips as they touched his skin made him burn with wanting. 'How could it be this intense?' He wondered.

Grace watched the desire move across Tavin's features and it spurred her on. As his fingers found her chin, she lifted her hand and lifted his fingers back to her lips. Her tongue tasted his flesh and the sensation drove her mad.

Tavin couldn't move. He could only sit there and watch as Grace kissed his fingers. It was like he wasn't there, more like he was watching a scene play out in front of him. The feelings her touch evoked were phenomenal in their intensity.

"Grace," Tavin whispered, "baby if you keep doing that, I'll forget about dinner."

Smiling, Grace looked up and met his eyes, "If you want me to stop, that's fine," she said and let his hand go from hers.

He wasn't expecting her to stop so suddenly so when she let go of his hand, it dropped into his lap with a thud. The motion was enough to knock some sense into him. What were they doing?

Grace watched him as he got up. He didn't look too sturdy and that made her smile. 'Good,' she said to herself, 'he needed to be as riled up as she was.'

Going into the kitchen, Tavin took deep breaths. Hell, she was only kissing his hand and it was like they already were making love.

He got the mushroom chicken dinner out of the oven and set out plates. It was the only dinner he made decently so he hoped Grace liked it. After fixing the plates, he put them on a tray and walked into the living room.

Seeing Grace, sitting in front of the fireplace with a dreamy look on his face, he felt a punch to his chest like he'd never experienced before. It scared the Hell out of him but it felt so…..right at the same time.

Grace looked up to see Tavin holding a tray with the oddest expression on his face. "Are you okay?" She asked, her voice laced with concern.

Tavin just nodded. He didn't know what was going on, he sure couldn't put it into words, and so he smiled and set the tray down.

"It smells wonderful," Grace said as he set the plates down.

Looking at her nervously, he said, "I should've asked if you liked mushrooms."

Smiling, Grace nodded, "Well, it happens that I do."

He was relieved. "Good," He said, "dig in."

It was amazing how different he could be. One minute he's all romantic and the next, he's just so brash. It was enough to test anyone's patience and Grace wasn't known for her patience.

Deciding it was better to just eat and figure it out as she went, Grace picked up her fork and took a bite.

"It's great," She said to Tavin.

The compliment made him feel warm. He was still reeling from whatever that was he felt when he walked into the room. Everything felt off kilter inside of him and he didn't know how to handle it. Maybe he was coming down with something because he didn't do these kinds of things.

He nodded in response and started eating.

They ate their meal while sitting in front of the fire. Grace couldn't help but feel like he was marking the time. His eyes never met hers, they darted around the room like he'd never been here before.

After they finished, Grace stood and was going to take her dishes into the kitchen when Tavin took her plate.

"I'll get these, you relax," He said.

The problem was, she couldn't. "I'd like to help you," She said.

Tavin shook his head, "No, I've got it." The words came out sharply. He could see their impact when Grace's smile faded. "I'm sorry," He mumbled and took the plates into the kitchen.

Grace plopped back down and took a gulp of wine, draining the glass. 'What were they doing here?' She wondered, very confused.

She filled her glass up again and drank it while staring into the fire. The wine was relaxing her and, she was pretty sure, that was the only reason she wasn't calling her aunt to come and give her a ride home. It was pretty clear Tavin didn't want her here.

He came back out to the great room a few minutes later to see Grace sitting in front of the fire just like earlier. The only difference was that she didn't look dreamy like before, she looked mad.

"Are you okay?" Tavin asked her.

Grace turned to look at him. His features were softened by the candlelight in the room, giving him a dreamy appearance. His voice was soft but his actions confused her. The alcohol was mellowing her so she said what she thought.

Frowning, Grace said, "Well, I don't know. You accuse me of whatever with Brandon, you cut me off when I ask where we're going, you make me feel all warm and crazy when we're sitting here, then you bring out dinner and make me feel like I'm intruding or something." She took a breath, "I wish you'd just make up your damn mind Tavin, do you want me or what?"

He couldn't process her words as fast as she said them but, when they did permeate his brain, he smiled and said, "I want you so much baby."

The words burst inside her in a hot rush. "Well, you have a really funny way of showing it," Grace mumbled.

Seeing her pout only made her more attractive. "Grace," He said and turned her so she was facing him. "Most of the time, I don't know what to do around you."

Her mouth opened as if she wanted to say something, but she didn't. She just stared at him.

"I'd be lying if I didn't say that our age difference wasn't a problem for me," He stated in agitation. "But it doesn't stop me from wanting to make love to you every time I see you."

Now Grace was really confused. He said he wanted her but told her there were issues. What were they supposed to do to get past those?

Tavin took her hands into his and kissed them. "Say something," He said in a breathy whisper.

Grace bit her lip, hesitated, then asked, "Would you get us some more wine?"

Nodding, Tavin stood to go into the kitchen for another bottle. 'Good thing Rich told him to get three of them.' He said to himself.

When he came back out a few minutes later, the bottle in his hand, Grace was nowhere to be found.

Chapter 14

Tavin's stomach fell to his feet. She was gone! Where could she have gone? She didn't have a car here. He looked around, thinking maybe she went to use the powder room but the door was standing open.

He was about to go out the front door when he heard a noise.

Turning quickly, he scanned the room. There, on the floor at the base of the stairs, was something. He rushed over and picked it up. It was her shirt!

He looked up the staircase, a smile forming. Slowly, he climbed the stairs. About four stairs up, he came across her shoes. At the top of the stairs, her pants were in a pile.

Walking down the hallway, he passed the rooms and knew, instinctively, that she would be in his. The door was open, as he always left it, and he stood in the doorway.

Seeing Grace sitting across the room in his overstuffed chair, in nothing but a bra and panties, his heart skipped a beat.

"What are you doing?" He asked in a husky voice.

Smiling, Grace leaned back in the chair and slowly crossed her legs. "I'm waiting for you," She answered.

Tavin took a few steps in and stopped when he reached the side of his bed. His fingers started undoing his shirt buttons.

Watching him watch her, Grace's insides were in a war between feeling nervous and aroused. She studied him as he removed his shirt, showing off his muscled shoulders.

"What are you doing?" Grace asked him, her voice sultry.

Smiling, Tavin took a step closer, "I'm getting ready to lift you up and put you in my bed," he said in a shaky voice.

The fact that he was nervous, made Grace happy. She didn't want to be the only one who had no clue as to what they were doing here.

She shifted in the chair, pulling her arm back behind her head and pulling her hair free from the clip she had it in for work. Her hair spilled down onto the chair behind her and draped down her shoulders, tickling her skin as it settled.

"And then what?" She asked, knowing the words were as intoxicating as the touch would be.

Tavin undid the top button of his jeans, "And then I'm going to lay down beside you and make love to you all night," he said clearly.

'What woman did not want to hear a man say those words to her?' Grace thought to herself.

"All night huh?" Grace questioned.

Nodding, Tavin took another step closer. He knelt down in front of her and ran his palm up the leg draped on top. When he reached her thigh, he gently pushed it off so he could kneel between her legs.

Without saying anything, Tavin ran his hands up Grace's arms. He slowly lifted them so that they would drape over his shoulders. Then he leaned in and kissed the crease of her neck where it touched her shoulders. The skin smelled of flowers and tickled his lips as they tasted it.

When Grace's head fell back to give him more access, he moved forward so her legs were on either side of his ribs and he could run his hands up her sides. He closed his eyes so he could focus on the way her skin felt underneath his fingertips.

"Ahhh," Grace breathed as his lips assaulted her senses.

Grinning, Tavin traced little circles across her shoulder with his tongue. If this was the only thing he needed for sustenance, he would be a happy man. Her skin melded with his as he moved closer still.

Grace could feel his chest hairs tickle her belly. She moved her hands up to rest in his hair, pulling it gently and running the tips of her fingers across his scalp.

Feeling his tongue on her skin was amazing! He switched to the other side and ran his hands up and down her ribcage. She strained against him, wanting more.

As Grace shifted, Tavin's arousal grew. It was straining against his jeans, creating a delicious friction. Although the ache inside of him would only be sated when he was buried deep inside of Grace.

"I need you," Tavin growled against her skin.

Smiling, Grace pulled back just far enough to look into his eyes, "Yes," she whispered.

She couldn't shake the feeling she was saying yes to more than sleeping with him though. The thought scared her and exhilarated her too.

Tavin stood and gathered her up into his arms as if she weighed nothing. He leaned down and kissed her deeply.

His tongue sparring with hers, along with being in his arms, comforted the restlessness inside of Grace. She felt as though she was meant to be here, in his arms.

They broke the kiss just long enough for Tavin to move the few steps from the chair to the bed.

Laying Grace down gently, Tavin ran his fingertips along her skin as he stood up beside the bed.

Grace watched in wonder as he removed his jeans. She lapped up the image of him standing above her as if she were thirsty and the sight of him was the only bit of water she could get.

He was beautiful, his muscles moving in perfect synchronicity with her mind. They flexed as he moved to lay on the bed beside her.

Tavin wanted to take it slow but the look in Grace's eyes told him she had something a little different in mind. They were dark, almost wild, as she looked him up and down.

"You are beautiful," Grace whispered.

He'd never had a woman say that to him before. The comment made him stop and look into her eyes. He wanted to say something but nothing formed in his mind. Instead, he smiled and moved his hand to take hers.

Grace looked at him in fascination as he placed her hand on his side and he ran his hands up the side of her, feeling every dip and swell of her body. When he reached her neck, her eyes looked up to meet his. She was enraptured by his gaze.

Still looking into Grace's eyes, Tavin moved his hands back down her body until he found the lace of her panties. With a quick tug, the flimsy fabric came apart and he moved her slightly to remove it.

Basically having her panties torn off was Grace's undoing. Never before, had she felt like this. She moved to straddle Tavin's belly. His hands came up to cup her breasts through the lace of her bra.

Tavin watched Grace above him, she was straddling his waist and he could feel the heat of her on his belly. He ached for her to slide down so he could fill her.

She felt emboldened and wanted to do everything physically possible with Tavin. His look made her feel alive and very safe at the same time. As if her wants were his, her thoughts, his, as if they were completely in tune.

Kneading her breasts as she moved over his belly, Tavin was pretty sure he wouldn't last very long this first time with her. The anticipation was building in leaps and bounds. Her nipples strained against the fabric of her bra, rubbing against the palms of his hands.

"Baby," He said hoarsely, "I need to be inside you."

Grace nodded and smiled. "Yes," She answered and stopped her movements against his belly.

Giving him a salacious look, Grace shifted so she was turned around.

Tavin didn't know what she was doing, only that he had the sexiest view of her bottom. His hands moved to cup her skin and massage it.

Grace was turned away from Tavin's face and focusing on the large bulge against his underwear. She pushed the fabric down slowly, allowing the tip of his arousal to peak above the fabric. The top of his sex was moist so Grace rubbed the tip of her finger across the head. She reveled in the way Tavin jumped at her intimate touch.

Once Grace touched his hardness, he couldn't wait. Half sitting up, he grabbed her waist and moved her over so she was on her back and he was kneeling between her legs.

His fast movement took her by surprise that faded into want as he perched himself above her.

"I've never wanted anyone this much," Tavin whispered to her.

A tear, slipped out of her eye and she prayed he didn't see it. Smiling, she arched up so her hips were touching his.

With a groan, Tavin shifted and pushed the tip of his hard sex deeply into Grace. When he was in as deep as he could be, he rejoiced in the knowledge that they fit perfectly together.

Grace's head flew back, "Oh Tavin," she groaned.

Having him fill her so completely was profound.

"Yes baby," He said back to her and started moving.

Their rhythm was not awkward and disjointed as it could be with first time lovers. Instead it was if they were completely in tune with one another. Reading each other as strongly as if they were long time lovers.

Tavin watched as Grace neared her climax, her eyes flew open and she stared up into his. His gaze intensified as he focused on bringing them both the release they were straining for, had been straining for since that first kiss four years ago.

The peak of climax climbing inside her, Grace smiled and let it wash over her like a tidal wave. Whoosh, she felt it crash against her insides and engulf her whole body with sensations she never felt before.

Her skin felt every contact with Tavin's. She could hear the sound of their mingled breaths as each of them was coming to grips with the enormity of their physical release.

Tavin watched her fall over the edge of reason and followed her closely. Seeing her climax made his heart stop......again......as it did before in the great room downstairs. Followed by his crash-like orgasm, he was falling into a deep well of satisfaction.

Tavin fell onto the bed beside her. Grace looked over at his face. His breathing was ragged, his eyes closed, his mouth set in a grin. She thought he was probably the most beautiful man in the world at that very moment.

When his eyes opened and looked into hers, it was like she was home. There would never be a more perfect moment than this one, Grace was sure of it.

"Hi," Tavin whispered.

Grace smiled, "Hi," she returned.

There was nothing else to say, nothing else he wanted to say. He wanted to lay here, with her tucked beside him, and wait for the rest of the world to just pass them by.

Tavin shifted to tuck her in so they were spooning. Feeling his body heat against her, she closed her eyes and immediately drifted off into sleep.

He lay there for a long time, listening to Grace's rhythmic breathing. She fell asleep quickly after their lovemaking. It took a lot out of him too but his fears kept him from following her into the lovely slumber his body craved.

She was so young. How did she even know what she wanted? And here he was, making love to her, knowing full well she wouldn't be staying here in Texas. He was borrowing trouble and heart ache and couldn't seem to stop himself from doing it.

Maybe this was a fluke? The amazing lovemaking was just some kind of strange kismet. He knew better but still tried to talk himself into believing it wasn't real.

"The hell it wasn't," He whispered to himself and closed his eyes.

Chapter 15

Grace woke up and didn't know why. There was a light on in the room so she was able to see. She was in Tavin's bed…..but he wasn't. The bathroom door off the room was open, the lights out so she assumed he wasn't in there.

Getting up, Grace looked for her clothes. Oh yeah, she stripped them off on her way upstairs. She tiptoed over to where Tavin threw his shirt and quickly put it on. It was big but smelled like him. Feeling it against her naked skin caused a jolt of desire to rush through her.

She smiled and walked out into the hallway.

There was no one there, the lights from the great room below lit the end of the hallway. About halfway down the stairs she could hear Tavin's voice.

"She's here with me," He said.

There was silence so she wondered if the other person was talking.

She padded across the floor and found him in the kitchen, her phone to his ear.

Tavin heard Grace's phone ring and got up to go downstairs and answer it.

It was her aunt, who figured that she was staying over but wanted to double-check.

He felt a little weird telling her aunt that she was spending the night when they really hadn't discussed it. He told her he was going to make love to her all night and she looked pleased by that but it wasn't exactly a yes.

"Hey," He said when he saw her standing in the doorway.

She looked young, standing there with his shirt on her frame. It engulfed her and made her look fragile.

Grace stood there and let him look at her. He had that odd look on his face again. She was smiling, however, because she wanted him again.

Tavin cleared his throat, "That was Melissa," he said.

Nodding, Grace walked over to him. "Uh huh," She answered and wrapped her arms around his neck.

"She wanted to know if you were coming home," He added as she kissed his bare shoulder.

She smiled at the hitch in his breath when her lips touched his skin, "And what did you tell her?" She asked.

It was damned difficult to concentrate when Grace was touching him and kissing him the way she was right now.

Tavin growled, "I told her you were here with me and you were staying here with me."

The tone of his voice was as strong as any aphrodisiac. It made Grace's body react in a multitude of ways.

"Really?" She asked, knowing she was playing with fire, and loving it.

Tavin set her away from him, he meant to be strong but one look at her and he was lost. Without thinking, he grabbed her and pulled her up onto him, her legs coming around him and crossing on his back.

His hands came around and cupped her bottom so she was crushed against him. The unbuttoned fly on his jeans allowing him to feel her heat against his crotch.

Grace's lips clamped on his, her mouth opening to take his with the force of the strongest siren. She kissed him roughly, wanting to feel every inch of him against her.

Tavin knew they weren't going to make it back upstairs, he was hard and wanted her even more than before. So much for the first release relieving his insatiable need.

He started walking toward the great room, with Grace wrapped around him. He made it to the far end of the room but misjudged where the doorway was and ended up crushing Grace against the wall.

"Tavin," Grace yelled, "I can't wait."

It was if her saying the words he was thinking was the permission he needed. Smiling against her mouth, he reached between them and pulled his throbbing hardness out of his pants. With a deft movement, he found her wet core and guided himself into her.

She was leaning against the wall and felt Tavin fill her. The movement made her eyes open wide in amazement. He was so hard! He filled her so completely that she had no idea where she ended and he began.

He could feel her hard bud of arousal push against the base of him and knew she was getting ready to cum.

"Yes baby," He whispered, "give it to me."

Grace threw her head back against the wall and struggled to push her pelvis into his. The need was welling up inside of her and she was helpless to keep it from rushing over her.

He pummeled her with his thrusts, wanting to wait until he knew she was cresting the edge before he followed. Once he felt her pulsing against him and felt her body tighten, he knew she was splashing over the edge and he followed her within a few more thrusts.

Minutes or hours later, Grace wasn't sure which, she finally opened her eyes to see Tavin looking at her with the most adorable face.

"Yes," She said smartly.

He smiled, "I was just thinking that seeing you in the midst of lovemaking is about the sexiest thing on earth."

The words embarrassed her for some reason. She blushed and shifted so he would put her down. Once her feet were on the floor, she tried to push her hair out of her face and find some semblance of balance.

Tavin could see she wasn't comfortable with his words yet. That didn't stop him from cupping her chin and lifting it up so she would look into his eyes.

He nodded his head toward the stairway, "Come to bed with me Grace, let me show you."

It was like being under a spell. Grace nodded and took the hand he offered her. They quietly walked upstairs and went to his bed.

She assumed he would start to make love to her again but, instead, Tavin tucked her in beside him. His fingers absently brushed her hair.

Hours later, Tavin woke to an empty bed. It was still dark outside. He looked at the clock, it was 3:47am and Grace wasn't beside him.

He didn't wait to pull on clothes, he just jumped out of bed to look for her.

The fire from the fireplace was bright. He came down the stairs and found Grace sitting in front of it. The glow from the flames lit her features. He could see the sheen of tears on her cheeks and a rush of panic ran through him.

Grace came downstairs, needing some space to breath. She woke up and saw Tavin beside her and was lost in the feel of him. It was like she was exactly where she was supposed to be.

Images of them sleeping together popped into her mind. Then a wedding, then kids, then she started to get anxious. They only slept together, they didn't profess love or commitment. She slowly got out of bed and came downstairs.

After putting more wood on the fire, she sat down on the blanket in front of the fire and let the tears fall down her face. They weren't sad tears, more like cleansing tears.

"Baby," Tavin whispered and felt bad that he startled her. "What are you doing down here?" He asked.

Grace saw that he was standing there without clothes and her body shifted straight into overdrive. What was it about him that made her respond so easily?

"I'm fine," She said with a meek smile. "I was just feeling a little unsettled."

Tavin nodded, "Did I do something wrong?" He asked. If he did, he'd fix it as soon as he could.

Grace's smile grew, he sounded like a kid. "No, you didn't," she waited as he sat down beside her. She touched his cheek with her palm, "I was just feeling a little overwhelmed."

It was hard to tell him things she couldn't explain to herself.

Tavin searched her face, she was scared, and he could see it. Nothing should ever scare her, not while he drew in breath.

Knowing that he didn't know what to say, Grace helped. "It's just that I know you have reservations about our age difference but," She looked at the fire, then back to him, "I've never felt that way with someone."

Tavin was torn between feeling arrogant that he was the only one to show her how lovemaking should be, and feeling sorry that any other previous lovers she had were probably just boys.

He couldn't bring himself to tell her that what they shared was profound for him as well. He didn't want to lead her on and confuse her any more than she already was. He nodded and leaned over to kiss her. If he couldn't say the words, at least he could show her how he felt.

He settled on the blanket, with his back against the ottoman and pulled her over so she was nestled in front of him.

Reaching up, Tavin pulled a blanket off of the couch and draped it over her.

Grace felt protected, he was around her, holding her tightly against his chest. The fire was in front of them, crackling and heating up; as if it mimicked her insides.

Tavin ran his hands up and down Grace's arms, enjoying the way her skin felt under his touch. They finally settled on her shoulders and massaged the muscles there. Her head lulled forward in relaxation and afforded him a view of her neck. Not being able to resist, he started to kiss the skin, loving the taste of her soft skin.

She was just melting under Tavin's touch and Grace knew that this would end with them making love. The inferno of need swept through her being with a force as strong as a tornado.

"Tavin," She whispered, "make love to me again."

Her words made him want to devour her and treasure her at the same time. He smiled against her skin and said, "Yes ma'am."

It was impossible not to smile at the way his words sounded. They were laced with a twang only he possessed.

His left hand grabbed her hair and swept it over her shoulder to give him more access to her sensitive skin. Leaning forward, he kissed her neck again but wrapped his hands around her body and cupped her breasts. Feeling the nipples jut out against his hands, he moved his fingers and flicked them with his thumbs.

The slow burn of desire increased into a firestorm of yearning Grace couldn't control, not that she even want to. She turned around within his embrace and got up on her knees. The movement brought her breasts up to his eye level. She offered first one, then the other to him.

Tavin feasted on her breasts, getting hard as he indulged each of them with his tongue.

"Yes," Grace said in a hiss of breath.

His responding groan told her he was with her in this.

Wrapping his arms around her, Tavin shifted them so she was now laying down and he was laid out beside her. The firelight played over her features making her appear as if she were a dream.

He ran his fingertips down her cheeks, "You are so tired, you should be asleep," he whispered as he dotted her face with kisses.

"As soon as you make love to me, then I'll sleep," Grace whispered.

Smiling, Tavin pushed up so he was above her, "Yes baby," he said.

Sinking into Grace's warmth was like feeling heat in an otherwise cold world. She made him feel strong and as if he alone could be the one to make her body sing with sexual tension.

This time their lovemaking was quiet, each of them sighing here and there. The focus was on discovering places and being wrapped up in their own world, if only for a little while.

Grace's climax was building slowly this time. She rejoiced in every sensation his touch created. She was beneath him, looking into his now-dark eyes, and wanted him to ride the crest of release with her.

Tavin watched her as he loved her, seeing the way his movements were matched by hers. Finding out what her body craved from his was extremely arousing. He wanted to please her but was getting too close to release as she arched up to force him deeper into her.

His face tightened, "Baby, I can't hold on," he said through gritted teeth.

Grace smiled, "Don't, give me everything," she yelled out and the thought of his orgasm forced hers to the surface.

With a final plunge, Tavin buried himself in her and let his body find the peak it was reaching for.

He watched Grace's face clench in her own release and it made him smile.

They collapsed into a pile, the blanket draped over them and the fire still raging in the fireplace. Its power only echoed what they were feeling on the inside.

Sleep claimed both of them quickly.

Grace slipped into a dream of her and Tavin. They were on horses and riding through the fields. The sun was shining and she felt warm and content. It was as if there were nothing stopping them from being happy.

Waking up hours later, Grace felt none of the heat from their lovemaking. She was alone on the blankets and Tavin was nowhere near her.

She got up, wrapping the blanket around her body and went in search of him.

He wasn't upstairs so she came back down and went into the kitchen. There was a note on the table. She picked up the paper and started to read it.

Grace,

Had to go out with Rich to check on some cattle. Didn't want to wake you. I've got Timmy waiting for you, he'll take you home.

TJ

Grace read the note twice, sure she was mistaken. He made love to her three times the night before and now he gets up and leaves her a note.

All the feelings she built up were drifting into the wind. 'How could he just write an impersonal note?' She asked herself.

'It was simple for him,' she answered herself. 'He doesn't feel the way you do apparently.'

She went upstairs to collect her clothes, tears streaming down her face as she went.

Chapter 16

Grace smiled at Timmy as he pulled into her aunt's driveway. She felt like some floozy and was embarrassed to be coming home in the morning.

She opened the door, "Thank you for the ride," she said quietly.

Timmy nodded, "My pleasure ma'am," he said sincerely.

He waited for her to walk inside the house before pulling away and wondered how much trouble his boss was in with the pretty lady.

Grace walked into her aunt's house and listened for any noises. She didn't hear anything and thought maybe Melissa was still asleep when she heard someone come down the hallway.

"Good morning," Melissa said brightly.

Her smile faded when she saw the look of hurt in Grace's eyes. She went up to her niece and hugged her.

Guiding her into the kitchen and gently urging her into a chair, Melissa went to pour them each a cup of coffee and asked, "Are you going to tell me why you look so upset?"

Tears started up as Grace told the story of what happened the night before.

Grace found herself sounding dreamy when she skimmed over the lovemaking. Her aunt didn't need to know the details. But the hurt refreshed itself when she talked about waking up alone and finding that ridiculous note.

Melissa listened to her niece, anger building with each revelation about Tavin.

After she finished, Grace sighed. "I'm going to go and shower so I can be ready for work," She said as she got up from the table.

"Take your time, we can go in a little late today," Melissa answered.

Grace nodded and left the room.

As soon as Melissa heard her niece's footsteps on the stairs, she picked up the phone and dialed. When the line connected, she said, "You'll never guess what that asshole of a friend your husband has did to my niece!"

Grace stepped into the shower and allowed the hot water to wash over her body. She hoped it washed away all the memories from the night before but knew nothing could erase them. Even if her mind shut it out, her body would remember each and every touch they shared.

She started crying. 'Why did he just leave?' She asked herself. 'Didn't he realize how that would make her feel?'

"I guess not," She said aloud.

An hour later, Grace was back downstairs and having a breakfast of toast. She couldn't stomach anything else right now.

Melissa eyed her niece up, "Honey are you okay?" She asked.

Grace nodded, "I will be," she answered quietly.

Smiling, Melissa knew her niece would recover but being hurt stung and being hurt twice by the same person hurt deeply. Personally she would be happy if Tavin McCormick got his ass handed to him. The nice thing was she knew just the two men to do the job.

Tavin was riding along the west side of the ranch, checking fences. Rich came into the house early this morning and found him with Grace on the floor in the great room.

Getting up, he told Rich to give him a minute and he went upstairs to get dressed.

When he came down, Grace was still asleep on the floor and he didn't want to wake her. She looked so beautiful, her hair mussed, and in a deep sleep.

He left a note for her so she could get home in time for work. Timmy seemed glad to make sure she got there safe.

Now, he was stuck. All he could think about was her and their time together the night before.

He wasn't even sure it was possible for someone to be this torn up over another person in such a short amount of time but, here he was, doing exactly that.

Rich was about 50 yards ahead of him, detouring some cattle away from a damaged fence.

Normally, the continuity of the ranch and the chores gave him peace. The only thing it gave him this morning was an ache to get back to Grace and he didn't like that one bit.

He turned around at the sound of approaching horses. It was a couple of riders from Seth's place.

Turning his mount, he trotted over to the fence where the riders could meet him.

After they got closer, he saw it was Seth and John riding. Good, he had some questions for Seth about some stock he was looking to invest in.

"Mornin," Tavin said and smiled.

He was greeted with silence. The look on both Seth's and John's faces was not good.

Sitting taller in his saddle, he waited for them to stop on the other side of the fence.

Seth pulled up his mount first and pointed at TJ, "You are lucky there's a fence between us McCormick," he started, "or I'd pull your sorry excuse of a man off that horse and whip your carcass like you deserve."

Tavin stared at his friend, completely lost about why Seth was mad.

John pulled his horse up to the fence, "Oh Seth, I'll take care of him if you like," he looked at Tavin with murder in his eyes, "you give men a bad name McCormick."

Interested in why three friends were yelling, Rich rode down the fence line up to where the others were standing.

"What's going on here?" Rich asked Tavin.

Shaking his head, Tavin turned to his foreman, "I've got no idea why they're so riled up Rich."

Getting off his horse, John was about to jump the fence that separated the men. Seth's hand on his shoulder stopped him short.

Seth, still looking pissed, wanted an explanation. Then they could beat the tar out of TJ.

He looked at Tavin and demanded, "You slept with Grace and then left her a note like she wasn't worth your time."

Doing a double-take, Tavin's jaw went slack. "What the hell are you talking about Rhodes?" He shouted back.

"That's it," John said through a clenched jaw, "I'll teach him a lesson," he said to Seth.

Rich positioned himself between John and Tavin. "Okay, okay, let's just simmer down here," He looked at John, "I came in early this morning because we had some trouble with the fence line and asked Tavin to give me a hand." He looked over at Seth, "I didn't know he had company until this morning."

Seth was starting to realize that the truth lie somewhere in the middle. Obviously, TJ's tone was not what Grace thought when she read the letter. If there was one thing he learned in the last year and a half about his wife, it was that his perspective and hers could be very different.

John, however, wasn't buying it. He heard the hurt in Melissa's voice and it made him angry as a steer during a round up.

Seth moved to take the reins of John's horse, "John," he said, "why don't we go on back home and explain to the ladies about the misunderstanding."

Reluctantly, John walked the few steps and threw himself up into the saddle of his horse.

The two men rode off quietly.

Once they were out of hearing range, Rich turned to Tavin, "I don't think John believed you," he said.

Nodding yes, Tavin responded, "I think you're right there." He turned his horse, "Let's wrap this up so I can get home and try to clear things up with Grace."

Rich watched his friend go back to work and smiled. After all this time, there was finally a woman who could wrangle him. It was about damn time too.

Grace went into work but holed herself up in Raelynn's office. She felt used and couldn't shake how awful that was. To her way of thinking, he got what he wanted, and just left the quickest way he could. She wondered, 'Is that how all rodeo cowboys behaved?'

The flowers he brought in the day before were in a vase on the credenza and every time she looked at them she felt a wave of regret.

She settled into her work and lost the minutes. The next time she looked up, her aunt was standing in the doorway with a look on her face Grace couldn't pin point.

"Are you okay?" She asked Melissa.

Melissa nodded and walked into the office. She closed the door behind her and sat down.

Clutching her hands together in nervousness, Melissa spoke. "I, uh, sort of told John what happened and he sort of rode over to TJ's place with Seth and sort of challenged him."

Grace stood up so quickly, her head spun. "What?" She asked, shocked that her aunt would do something like that.

"In my defense," Melissa started, "I was just hurting for you."

Thoughts were whirling through Grace's mind. She did actually appreciate her aunt's concern but she was an adult now. If he thought she was a mere child before, what must he think now?

Pacing the office, Grace turned to her aunt and asked what she was thinking, "What does he think of me now?"

There was a noise at the door and both women turned to see Tavin standing there.

"He thinks that your family loves you very much and that jackass should have escorted you home himself." His words were tight with stress. He hoped Grace didn't sent him packing.

Melissa stood and looked from Tavin to her niece and back again. 'Oh,' She thought, 'there is something big going on there.'

Clearing her throat, Melissa moved to the door, "I'll let you two talk and I'll lock up so just go out the back door when you leave."

She left the office and hoped the emotion she saw on her nieces face wouldn't change anytime soon.

Grace stood where she was and didn't move. She had no clue what to say to him.

Tavin moved into the office. 'Was he here only last night?' He asked himself.

"I was thinking that I owed you a pretty big apology." He said softly and took another step toward Grace. "I read the note I left and it was cowardly."

Shaking her head no, Grace smiled weakly, "I am so sorry my aunt's friends were bullying you."

Tavin smiled, "I think I can handle Seth but John, he was pretty riled up." He said.

Embarrassment flooded Grace's cheeks. She clasped her hands together and said, "I bet you think I'm some immature kid again."

Her statement surprised him. Tavin was under the impression that last night was pretty spectacular and they turned a corner. Being with her squelched any doubts he had about her being some "kid."

"I'm pretty sure," He said and stopped in front of her, "that a "kid" wouldn't have made love with me like that."

His words were doing that weird thing that turned her insides into a doughy mess. Warmth filled her and it wasn't from embarrassment anymore.

Feeling brave, she spoke up and asked, "Is that what you think we did, made love?"

Reaching out, Tavin cupped her cheek into his palm, "Oh yes, Miss Grace, that is exactly what we did." He answered.

"Then," Grace said as she stepped closer and wound her arms around his neck, "Let's see what we can do to clarify any misgivings either of us have."

His smile brightened, "I'm all for clarification," he said as he lowered his lips to hers.

The kiss started out gentle, with each of them shifting so they were tangled in one another's embrace.

Grace hummed with excitement. His lips moved over hers as if they were made for each other.

Tavin moved his hands up and filled his palms with her soft hair. The strands caressed his skin and added another layer to his awareness.

Pulling away, Tavin took in a deep breath. It wasn't from kissing her, it was from her being so near that she made him forget to breath.

"I think if we don't stop now, your aunt is going to know what we were doing." Tavin said softly.

Grace nodded, "I understand," she left his arms and picked up her bag, "let's get out of here," she said as she grabbed his hand and led him out of the office.

Chapter 17

Tavin drove Grace to her aunt's house and sat with her in his truck talking.

"I'm sure Melissa would be fine with you coming in," Grace said, reluctant to leave him.

The connection they shared last night was back and Grace was leery about breaking it again.

Dropping his forehead so it was touching hers, Tavin held her hands in his.

He sighed, "I think it's best if I drop you off, as a gentleman should," he said.

Grace understood what he was saying logically but her body wanted a completely different outcome.

With a final kiss that took their respective breaths away, she smiled and opened the door to get out of the truck.

"Wait!" Tavin rushed out.

Looking at him, she wondered what he was doing. He jumped out of the driver's side and ran around to her side of the truck and helped her down.

He took her arm and walked her up to the door.

Grace imagined that not that many women were able to say that about their lovers.

Tavin looked at Grace, the dim light from the street lamp left half of her face in shadow. Even so, she was still beautiful. He could stand there and just look at her for hours.

They kissed once more, less passionate than earlier but it still impacted Grace in a way she couldn't really explain.

Tavin moved away and the only contact between them was their joined hands, "Come to the ranch tomorrow and we'll go riding," he said with a smile.

Grace nodded, "I'll try to get out a little early so it's still light out," she answered.

He released Grace's hand and walked down the steps of the porch. Before he got to his truck he turned around and said, "I'll see you tomorrow Grace."

The words warmed her when his physical absence left her feeling cold. She nodded and went inside. Leaning against the door as she listened for his truck to pull out of the driveway, Grace smiled.

"Did you get things worked out?" Melissa asked her niece when she walked into the hallway to see Grace leaning against the front door looking dreamy.

Grace nodded yes. "I'm going to ask to cut out early tomorrow, Tavin is taking me riding," she blurted out quickly.

'Ahhh, first love,' Melissa thought. She wouldn't give it a second thought except for the fact that Tavin was so much older than Grace. She worried for her niece and hoped he didn't hurt her like he did this morning. Grace wasn't one for playing games so if he thought she was, he was in for a rude awakening.

"I think something can be arranged," Melissa answered and headed into the kitchen.

Grace went upstairs to change into more comfortable clothes.

When she came down a few minutes later, she saw her aunt hanging up the phone.

Looking a little bit like a mom, she asked, "Are you done relaying the latest gossip about my love life?"

Melissa laughed, "Maybe," she replied flippantly. "I need something to keep me busy."

Shaking her head in exasperation, Grace pointed to her aunt, "You have your own love life to be preoccupied with."

"You're right," Melissa answered with a smile. "Speaking of which," She added, "I think I'll go change and wait for my sweet cowboy to show up. It's a movie night."

Watching her aunt walk out of the room, Grace smiled. Oh the women and their tangled webs of chaos in relationships. 'No wonder men think we're all nuts, we pretty much are.' She said to herself.

After making a quick meal of soup and a grilled-cheese sandwich, Grace went upstairs to her room and checked her Facebook page.

There was a message from Hailey asking how she was doing in Texas.

Grace wrote a quick note back saying that things were going pretty well. She briefly mentioned seeing Tavin, or TJ as Hailey called him, and told her friend that her mom looked great.

It was nice to think about other things, even if it was only for a few minutes.

She scanned the pictures Hailey posted and laughed at the faces she and her friends made during their trip across Europe. They were currently in Rome and seemed to be having a great time.

After posting a few responses to her friends' posts, Grace closed her laptop. She turned on the tv and let the sound of it drown out her thoughts.

Was it only last night that she spent the night at Tavin's making love? She allowed the thoughts of their lovemaking wash over her. Unfortunately that aroused her to a point where she called his cell phone.

The phone rang twice before he picked up. "Hello," Tavin said sharply.

He was working on some ranch financial documents and they always ticked him off. He couldn't figure out how paperwork could make someone feel so stupid!

"Hey there," Grace said softly into the phone.

Hearing Grace's voice, Tavin turned away from his desk and smiled. "Hey, I'm sorry, I was looking over documents and was getting frustrated," he said.

"Well," She responded, "I was thinking about you and me and last night and I was getting frustrated too."

Oh, the game was started! Tavin chuckled, "I'm thinking we're talking about two distinctive kinds of frustration," he ran his fingers through his hair, "and I sure like yours better," he added.

Grace harrumphed, "I'll just bet," she said dryly.

Now he laughed. "What?" He asked, "You don't believe me?"

She loved how the tone of his voice changed. "I guess," She teased.

"Don't make me come over there," Tavin said, only half-teasing.

That made Grace laugh, "That's exactly what I'm trying to get you to do," she answered.

At this rate, Tavin was pretty sure he wouldn't get any more paperwork done tonight. Not that he particularly cared. Hearing Grace's voice trumped it all.

He stood up and walked out of his home office and into the great room. The blankets they used last night were still lying on the floor in front of the fireplace. The memories started to fill his mind and he let them. Just one night with her was better than any he could remember.

"I hope you don't mind," Grace started, "but I mentioned that you and I were 'seeing one another' to Hailey." She hesitated before adding, "Is that okay?"

Tavin smiled, she was sweet. "Are we seeing one another?" He asked intentionally being feisty.

Grace's eyes narrowed. He was teasing her. "I suppose you could categorize it that way," She said.

He could feel the conversation turning onto a more serious path and he didn't want to do that now. Their relationship was too new.

"Then I don't mind," He answered in a light tone.

Grace wanted to let him know she knew her role in their misunderstanding as well. "I promise that I'll try to keep prying relatives out of our business as well." She said with a smile.

Her tone was lighter and that made Tavin feel relief.

"Yeah," He answered, "I think I was really only seconds away from having the tar beat out of me today." Sighing, he added, "But I can understand how John felt."

Her interest piqued, Grace asked, "You can?"

"Sure," Tavin answered. "Men are protective of their women, he was only reacting to Melissa's concern for you."

The way he said "their women" rubbed Grace a little raw. He said the words like men owned women, or at least that's the way Grace took it. She knew she should give him a break, he was trying to make up for the miscommunications but she was still feeling a little unsettled by it all.

Shutting off the tv, Grace stifled a yawn and said, "I think I'll let you go, I'm getting tired. Thank you for talking to me."

Tavin listened to her and felt like there was a subtle change in her tone. He wondered if he misspoke again. She didn't sound mad so he discounted it as his own paranoia.

"Okay baby," He used the endearment he started last night, "you sleep well and I'll see you tomorrow."

Grace smiled when she heard the word, 'baby.' It made her feel as if she were important to him.

She sighed, "Good night."

Tavin hung up the phone and couldn't quite settle himself down for a while afterwards. She was young and maybe she didn't have the experience or maturity in relationships he had.

Sitting on her bed, Grace wondered if Tavin understood what she thought. You didn't spend time making love like they did last night unless it was important. At least that's what she hoped.

The next morning, Gràce beat the alarm clock. She was dressed and ready before Melissa even had her first cup of coffee, which was unheard of before.

She even had her riding clothes in a bag near the front door so she could leave work and go directly to Tavin's ranch.

"I'm going to take my own car into the office so I can leave early," Grace said as Melissa sat at the table and tried to get going.

Melissa nodded and grumbled, "That's fine."

Grace smiled. Her aunt was not a morning person until the first cup of coffee was running through her system.

They got to the office a little earlier than usual and Grace jumped into her duties. She got through three particularly lengthy files before lunchtime and was confident they were reviewed and specific notations were made.

Grace asked if she could work through lunch so she could leave early and Melissa agreed.

Cleaning up the office, Grace smiled absently, thinking about Tavin. The smile faded when she saw the ever-persistent and annoying, Brandon in the doorway.

"Yes?" She asked him coolly.

Brandon cocked his head, "I was just wondering if you'd changed your mind about going out with me?" He asked.

Grace could absolutely not believe his audacity. "Uh, no," She replied.

He nodded and left the doorway.

After she was finished, she went into Melissa's office and said goodbye. As she was leaving through the back door, she ran into Brandon again. Only this time, he was positioned in front of the doorway.

"Brandon," She said with more confidence than she felt. "Please move."

He did as she asked so Grace was relieved. She walked past him and out to her car. It was when she was pulling away that she saw him staring at her with a very intense look in his eyes. It unsettled her but she wasn't going to worry about him right now. She was happy to push everything out except thoughts of Tavin.

An hour later, she and Tavin were on horses and walking along fence line on Tavin's ranch. He was even sweet enough to ask Seth if he could use Cindy for Grace. The gesture was very kind and touched Grace.

"Why do some people call you TJ?" Grace asked him as the question popped into her mind.

Tavin smiled, "My given name is Tavin Joseph and my mom was always calling me Tavin Joseph when I was growing up because I was usually getting into some trouble." He looked at Grace and continued, "I guess she got tired of saying the whole name after a while and shortened it to TJ."

The explanation was crazy, but Grace was pretty sure it was true. "Oh," She answered.

Grace asked him, "What would you like me to call you?"

He thought about it for a moment and answered, "I like the way Tavin sounds when you say it so I'd have to say I'd prefer that."

She nodded, "Okay then."

They rode a little further before she asked, "When did you first notice me?"

This was an easy question for Tavin to answer, "I first saw you at the diner in town, then again at the lake."

She opened the can of worms now, so Grace asked the next logical question, "So did you mean what you said about kissing me?"

Tavin turned in his saddle so he could look at Grace. He measured his words before he used them.

"Grace," He said softly. "I have no reason at this point to lie to you." He took her hand in his and nudged his horse into moving again. "I told you what I thought."

She nodded. "I'm sorry if my asking upset you."

He stopped his horse again so he could look at her. "Baby, I'm not upset." He looked around them at the fields on his land, then back to her eyes, "I can't rightly explain something I don't 100% understand but I can say, I wanted you…..still want you."

Grace watched the look of sincerity in his eyes and knew she could accept what he gave for now.

Chapter 18

They rode until dusk set in. The horses walked side by side and you could hear the leather of the saddles move with them. It was very relaxing to Grace's system. After the craziness of the last week, she needed a way to even out her feelings.

He answered all of Grace's questions, even if they were silly ones about the ranch. She appreciated his patience. Surprisingly, he asked a few questions of his own; about Grace's college experience, what she wanted to do after she graduated. It was probably very boring to others, but, to her, it was wonderful.

They were on their way back to the barn when Tavin asked, "Would you like to stay for dinner?"

Grace hoped he would want to extend their time together; she sure did.

"Yes," She answered, "that would be great."

He nodded and continued to ride for a few minutes more before he added, "I, uh, don't have any other recipes so we'll have to order in."

That made Grace laugh, "Okay," she said, "we can check to see if there's something in your kitchen salvageable."

A few minutes later, they arrived at the barn and unsaddled their horses. After the cool down, they put the horses in their stalls and walked up to the house.

Grace took the time to look at his house. It was very large for one person. It was beautiful, but the sheer size piqued her curiosity.

"How long have you lived here?" She asked Tavin.

He thought for a moment, then answered, "About ten years now," he started, "I bought it with one of my first rodeo purses."

That comment made her think of other things she wanted to ask.

He opened the back door and let her precede him inside. They took off their jackets and hung them up in the mud room. Grace peeked around as they walked through.

The laundry room was right off of the mud room and then they were in the kitchen.

Grace noted that it was very spacious and rather modern. The outside of the house was designed to make it look older but the inside was definitely updated.

Tavin looked in the refrigerator and frowned. "Not much in there," he said.

Joining him, Grace smiled, "There is plenty of food in here," she poked at him playfully, "we'll whip something up."

Looking at Grace, Tavin smiled. She may be a lot younger than him, but she knew more than he did about a lot of things. Maybe their age difference wasn't as bad as he thought.

Pulling out some vegetables and some left-over steak from the frig, Grace threw together the fixings for fajitas. She laughed at his puzzled look when she asked where he kept the spices.

"I'll figure it out," She finally said and dug out a fry pan.

After twenty minutes, they were seated at the table in the kitchen. Tavin took a bite and thought he was in heaven.

He looked at Grace, "Woman you can cook!" He said enthusiastically.

His comment made Grace beam. Of course, she'd never admit that it was an easy recipe. Instead she smiled and ate her food.

After dinner they cleaned up the dishes and went into the great room. Tavin was looking for the remote for the television when Grace spied a photo album on one of the end tables.

She gestured to the book, "Do you mind?" She asked Tavin.

He shrugged and, finding the remote, turned on the tv.

Grace sat down on the sofa, loving the way the leather shifted and creaked with her movements. It reminded her of being on horseback; comfortable.

The photo album was actually a scrapbook. It contained news clippings and pictures of Tavin from when he was a little boy to recently. She looked up and found him staring at her.

"My mom put it together," He offered.

Smiling, Grace went through the album again from the beginning. "You were so cute," She would say, prompting a snort from Tavin.

He frowned, "What do you mean were?"

Grace chuckled, "You are handsome now, you've moved way past cute."

Nodding, Tavin said, "Good save."

He sat down beside her and started pointing out articles and adding information.

It was so easy to sit there and listen to his stories.

The only thing Grace was leery about was when he would mention injuries. His tone always played them off as no big deal. She remembered hearing about a rodeo participant being killed last year in the news. For all his blasé comments, she thought he was sugar-coating the kind of work he did.

"Are you going to retire?" She asked.

The word didn't sit well with Tavin. At his age, most men were out of the circuit but he felt like he had a few more years left. He was ranked high in the standings and qualified for Nationals so he didn't think "retiring" was in the cards just yet.

He looked over to see Grace patiently waiting for his answer.

"In a couple of years," He said, "I'll be done with it."

His answer sounded very final so she didn't ask him any more questions.

She put the scrapbook back on the table and they settled in to watch a movie. Grace tried to pay attention but there was a niggling of something in the back of her mind.

Days later, that feeling was still there and Grace couldn't pinpoint what the problem was.

Tavin spent time with her almost every day now. They were officially dating and things were great; except that little hiccup of doubt she kept jammed in the back of her mind.

She had no clue what it was about, just that it was there.

Tavin told her that the National Rodeo Finals were in three weeks in Las Vegas and he was starting to get ready for it.

Thanksgiving was next week and she was trying to help Melissa get everything ready since they were hosting it at the house. Seth, Raelynn, John, and a couple of the hands who didn't have other plans were coming over. Grace mentioned it to Tavin the day before but he was non-committal and changed the subject.

His behavior only added to the worries she carried about their relationship. She tried, very hard, not to "borrow trouble" as her mother put it but it was tough.

On Friday, Melissa came into the office and announced that everyone got to get off early. The Lake Jackson Festival of Lights was starting and everybody could go if they wanted.

As a gift to the interns and Grace, Raelynn and Melissa got everyone tickets for ice skating. It was a silly thing but it touched Grace that they would think of it.

Since she hadn't heard from Tavin for the last two days, he was in the Dallas area working on a deal for cattle, so she decided she'd go with Amy. Her aunt already said that she and John would be going but Grace kind of felt like a 3rd wheel around them.

She and Amy planned on getting seats for the parade that evening and left work early to scope out the spot they wanted. Amy rented an apartment in Angleton so she went home to change and Grace put their chairs in place and held the spot until she came back.

Pulling out her tablet, she started reading a book she wanted to read for a while. The weather was chilly but not "Cold" so she wrapped up in a blanket and started reading.

She was well into the story when a noise got her attention. As she looked up, Grace saw Tavin standing beside her.

Surprised, her breath caught and then she said, "Hello there."

Once Tavin got into town, he headed straight for Melissa's office. Hell-bent on seeing Grace, he didn't even go home to change.

Without speaking, he bent down and kissed Grace.

His lips fit hers perfectly and Grace was drawn into his warmth. Their lips melded first and then their tongues touched. Ahhhh, this was what she needed, to feel him.

Tavin knew a kiss wouldn't be enough for him. He stood back up and brought her with him. His arms went around her body and held her to him tightly.

Breathing was hard and it wasn't because Tavin was holding her tight, it was because he took it away with his kisses. Even though they'd kissed hundreds of times by now, it always felt like the first one. Her heart raced and her mind blurred.

When Tavin finally released her, he wished they weren't standing on a public street. He'd rather have Grace at his house and in his bed.

"How was your trip?" Grace asked, trying to find some semblance of clear brain function.

Tavin smiled, "It was lucrative," he answered. "I wanted to get back here."

The words he spoke always sounded like they were about her but he'd stop just short of actually admitting it.

Pushing the doubts away, she nodded. "Good."

He watched Grace sit back down and wondered if he said something wrong. She wasn't unhappy to see him, if the kiss was any indication, but she wasn't...... He couldn't say exactly.

People were now starting to line the parade route. Traffic was picking up with people trying to find parking before the streets were closed.

Tavin was feeling out of place, just standing there. "Are you going to the festival after the parade?"

Nodding, Grace grabbed her tablet and shut it down since she didn't think she could go back to reading after that kiss.

"Amy and I are going," She said.

Tavin took the words to mean that he was officially NOT invited.

He tried not to be let down by her words and asked, "Do you want to call me when you're done?"

Grace smiled, she hoped he would want to see her. "Yes," She responded.

Feeling like he should get going, but not wanting to, Tavin said, "Okay, I'll talk to you later."

Nodding again, Grace smiled and watched him walk across the street and get into his truck.

Something about their conversation was off.

Half an hour later, Amy showed up and Grace put the awkward reunion with Tavin behind her. The parade was starting as soon as it was dark and the route was now jam packed. The festival was a pretty big deal here.

The floats started to come down the street and the girls oohed and aahed over the lights. Some of the floats were funny, some were inspirational, and some were downright breathtaking.

It was fun to wave to the participants and laugh at the shenanigans of people determined to have fun. There were street vendors selling glow in the dark necklaces and different little toys.

After the parade was done, they picked up their folding chairs and stuck them in the trunk of Grace's car. The festival was only a few blocks away so they walked over.

Amy liked the craft displays so they spent a lot of time going through the small tents. It was fun to see some of Amy's shyness dissipate. She was a very nice girl but the wallflower bit overshadowed that.

"Did you want to get something to eat?" Amy asked as they came to the food vendors.

Grace shook her head no, "I'm going to call Tavin in a few minutes. He's back in town."

Nodding in understanding, Amy commented, "He's crazy about you, I wish someone would be crazy about me."

The wistfulness in Amy's voice made Grace feel low. If what her new friend said, then how come she felt so disjointed about Tavin?

Trying to downplay it, Grace said, "We're just dating."

Although Amy didn't comment right away, Grace had the impression she didn't believe Grace's words.

They walked for a while longer, poking around the various vendors' tents. It was nice and kept Grace's mind preoccupied.

After they went through the main aisle of displays, Amy met up with some other friends from school. Grace hugged her quickly and told her to have a good time.

Once she got back into her car, she called Tavin's cell phone.

She frowned when it went to voicemail. "Hey," She said when the recording asked her to leave a message, "It's me. Give me a call when you can."

Hanging up, she figured she might as well go home and get some food. She assumed she would eat with him but now…..she didn't know.

Chapter 19

Tavin grabbed his phone when he heard it ring but it already went to voicemail. He saw that it was Grace and cursed.

He tried to call her back but got a busy signal.

The day started out good since he knew he was going home and would see Grace. Then when he saw her it was like all of his hopes dropped down to his feet. She seemed distant and not as happy to see him as he was to see her.

Maybe she realized he was too old for her? Maybe she was thinking she didn't want some rodeo guy? The doubts sprouted up in his mind like crab grass in his fields. They were stubborn and were damned difficult to get rid of.

Once he was back at the house and cleaned up, he tried to call her again. His patience was held on by a thread and he was anxious for her to pick up. He sighed in relief when she did.

"Hello," Grace said.

She knew it was Tavin because of caller ID but she was still upset that he didn't answer earlier.

Tavin smiled, "Hi, I'm sorry I missed your call earlier, I was in the barn and didn't hear my phone."

His reason seemed plausible so Grace relaxed. "That's fine," She said, "you got back to me."

She meant it. Hearing his voice made her insides turn to the consistency of oatmeal and she'd forgive him just about anything.

"Come over," Tavin said in a raspy voice.

Normally he would cover it up but, with Grace, he didn't care if he sounded needy. He was.

Grace smiled, "I'll leave now," she answered.

After disconnecting the call, Grace walked downstairs and out the door. She was in her car and headed to Tavin's in record time.

He was waiting on the porch when she got there and he looked.....desperate, in Grace's opinion. Of course she was desperate herself; desperate to have his hands on her, his lips on her, whatever he would give her, she would take.

She put the car in park and got out. For a second, she stopped and looked at him. He stood there in jeans, a t-shirt, and boots, backlit by the porch lights. Her cowboy!

Grace moved then, faster than she thought she could. She was up the stairs and in his arms, the force of them coming together drove Tavin backwards into the front of the house.

Tavin couldn't think. She was in his arms and he was pushed back against the brick façade of the house and he didn't care.

Her lips were all over his face and neck, her hands were pulling up on his t-shirt. His lips tasted her ear lobe and neck and his hands were on her back, holding her to him.

"I missed you," Grace whispered as she kissed him.

The words eased his earlier doubts. Smiling, he said, "I missed you too."

They managed to get into the front door but Grace couldn't remember how. She was too focused on kissing him and touching him.

Her hands ran up and down his back as she kissed him deeply. She scratched her nails over his skin and reveled in the thought that she would leave her mark on his body.

Tavin was pretty sure that he wouldn't be able to get her upstairs into his bedroom. He wanted her too much.

Groping for furniture so he wouldn't trip them both and fall on the floor, Tavin maneuvered them so they made it to the sofa.

He sat down and pulled Grace down so she was straddling his lap.

They kissed until neither of them could breathe.

Grace was panting from lack of oxygen and the need coursing through her body at the speed of light.

'Oh, he felt so good!' She repeated over and over in her mind.

"Baby," Tavin growled when he couldn't take another minute without burying himself inside her, "take off your pants."

Still managing to kiss him, Grace slid off his lap so she was next to him. Blindly, she undid the snap and zipper of her jeans and pushed them down, along with her panties.

As soon as Tavin realized she was exposed, he moved his hand to cup her intimately. Heat poured out from her now-ready sex. He parted her with his fingers and dipped first, one, then two fingers inside her and cursed at how ready she was for him.

Grace pulled away just long enough to get her pants the rest of the way off. She watched as Tavin didn't bother to take his off, just undid them and pushed the fly aside so she had access to what she needed. She ran her hand the length of him, purring with female satisfaction.

Tavin's voice was hoarse when he said, "Now baby," to her.

Straddling him again, Grace sighed as she settled over him and slid down his shaft. The feeling of him filling her slowly was better than anything else she could think of. It took control for her not to topple over into an orgasm.

The slowness in which Grace sheathed him with her hot, heat was a pure form of madness in Tavin's mind. He watched her face as it contorted with pleasure. When they were completely joined, she sighed and that was almost his undoing.

Tavin slid down on the sofa a little more, creating even more delicious, friction between them.

Grace stopped and looked into his eyes. They reflected the fireplace with the sparks flying across his pupils. She could understand now what pure hunger meant.

Then, as if time started again after stopping completely, she began moving over him. Slowly at first, wanting to feel every inch of him as he moved within her.

Placing his palms so they were cupping Grace's breasts, Tavin's breathing was ragged. The woman could undo him in every sense of the word in a matter of minutes.

"Are you ready?" Grace asked slowly, inflecting her tone with a sultry sound.

Not able to form coherent words, Tavin could only nod.

Her rhythm increased, burning them both up in an inferno of raging lust.

Tavin moved his hands down Grace's sides and settled them on her hips. He wanted to control her movements in an attempt to prolong his release.

"No," Grace yelled into the room, "I want it faster Tavin!"

She fought him and she would win, he knew it and she knew it. Throwing his head back, Tavin let her ride him in abandon until he could see her orgasm coming. She licked her lips and started to tense as her body accepted the pummeling of sensations.

"Yes," Tavin yelled, "Give it to me, Grace!"

Within seconds, he was joining her on the wild ride to the erotic beyond. The waves of electrical pulses assaulted his system so much that any further words were not possible.

Grace collapsed onto Tavin's chest, her own heaving in synchronicity with his. Her smile was against his skin and she knew that this was as powerful for him as it was for her.

A long while later, when they were recovered enough to move and speak, Grace leaned back. Her smile reflected her body; sated.

Tavin looked up and thought that she would never look as beautiful as she did when he thoroughly loved her.

"You look like the proverbial Cheshire Cat," Grace whispered as she leaned in and kissed the tip of Tavin's nose.

Tavin smiled, "I think that's like the pot calling the kettle black don't you thing?" He asked, teasing.

Grace nodded, "Yep," she said and shifted.

When they weren't connected, Tavin felt a little lost. Funny, she was right here and yet he didn't like not touching her.

His arm snaked out and grabbed her quickly, pulling her onto his lap so he could kiss her deeply.

Laughing at his playfulness, Grace embraced it. After their earlier distance, this was what they needed. At least in Grace's opinion.

"Are you hungry?" Grace asked him.

His eyes let her know he meant something other than food so she playfully punched him in the arm.

Getting up, Grace swatted his hands as they tried to get her into his lap again. "I meant for food," She said dryly.

Tavin nodded, "Yes." He answered.

"Pizza!" Grace said and walked over to where her purse was thrown on the floor.

She called a local place in Alvin and placed her order. When she hung up the phone, she turned around and smiled at Tavin.

"We have 25 minutes," Grace said slowly.

Before Tavin could respond, she ran over and hopped onto his lap. He laughed at the look on her face, it was sweet and mischievous.

They decided against another round of lovemaking, instead opting to get dressed and get a fire going in the fireplace.

The pizza arrived on time. Tavin got paper plates out of the kitchen with some napkins and they sat down on blankets in front of the fire and ate.

Grace smiled as she bit into the slice of pizza, its gooey cheese tasting better than a steak dinner. She realized how hungry she was and laughed.

"What?" Tavin asked.

Winking at him, Grace said, "You give me a big appetite."

The double meaning wasn't lost on him. He could feel the stirrings inside and wondered if he would ever stop reacting to her like this. There were relationships over the years; a few of them serious. For some reason, he never could stay and he didn't understand why……. Until now.

Grace could see him thinking about things. The change of facial expressions was interesting in the firelight. He was interesting. For as many issues as they had, being with Tavin made her feel content and that wasn't something people found every day.

Now, though, it was about figuring out if he felt the same way or if he was just interested in the here and now.

"I guess we're both wondering about things," Tavin spoke up.

Being tossed back into reality, Grace smiled, a little embarrassed at being caught.

She nodded, "I guess."

He didn't want things to be awkward between them so he asked, "I don't think I've ever asked you what you plan to do after college?"

Another question she didn't know the answer to. She reverted back to the stock answer she gave everyone when they asked that question.

"Well," She said, "I'm hoping to get on with a company as an advisor."

'Cryptic,' Tavin thought, 'and PC.' He wondered if she really had a clue.

Gathering up their plates, he stood to take them into the kitchen. She got up and grabbed the pizza box and followed him.

He threw the plates into the trash, "I was sure I was going to school to be a lawyer," he said.

Grace was so shocked that she just stood where she was, the pizza box frozen in her hand.

When Tavin turned around, he almost laughed at the shocked expression on Grace's face.

"Don't look so surprised," He said dryly.

Grace shook herself out of her gaze, "Oh sorry," she said. "I just never thought of you as a lawyer."

Tavin nodded, "I was on the Dean's list at UT for pre-law."

Feeling silly, Grace smiled, "Here, I didn't realize I was in the company of greatness." She walked over and kissed him.

He appreciated her effort in lightening the mood and kissed her back.

"What changed your path?" Grace asked when she stepped back to put the pizza box in the refrigerator.

Grabbing the wine bottle off the counter, Tavin walked back into the living room with Grace. He had to really think about what his answer was.

They sat down and Tavin poured the wine into their glasses before saying, "I did rodeo since I was old enough to walk and always thought it would be a way to make money for school."

Grace nodded and smiled.

"I graduated and was looking at law schools and came to the realization that I didn't want to practice, I wanted to ride rodeo and that wasn't going to change," He said with a half-smile.

Grace couldn't help but think he looked like a little kid in the way he was dreamy about his chosen career. As dangerous as it seemed to be, at least he was doing what he loved. That was more than she could say.

"I guess," She said as she took a sip of wine, "I'm just trying to make the right choices."

This is where their age difference was apparent. He remembered being in that same place. Maybe he could help her with his experience.

Putting his glass down, Tavin looked into the fire, "Just figure out what makes you happy and follow that," he said and looked over at Grace.

Her hair fell over her shoulders, still mussed from their lovemaking. He reached up and finger-combed the strands.

Grace sighed, "Right now," she started, "you make me happy."

The statement, although said lightly, made him feel weighed down in emotion. Not wanting it to be like that, he turned and took her glass from her hand. Placing it on the table, he took her into his arms and kissed her.

Chapter 20

Thanksgiving Day arrived and Grace was up early helping her aunt with the turkey. They laughed as they talked about the holiday experiences in the past. Melissa talked about how her sister, Grace's mother, had burnt the turkey the first year she made it.

"Oh, remember the year dad cut into it and found the bag of gizzards?" Grace asked as they stuffed the bird.

Melissa laughed, "Oh we had to go out to eat that year." She said and scrunched her face with the memory.

They put the turkey in the oven and Melissa blew out a breath, "There," she said, "the hardest part is done."

Grace put up her hand to high-five her aunt. "Now what?" She asked.

Going over to the refrigerator, Melissa pulled out a bottle of champagne and lifted it up, her eyebrows winking.

"How about a mimosa?" She asked her niece.

Laughing, Grace went to the cabinet to get out two glasses, she gave them to Melissa.

After they poured the drinks, they sat down at the table.

A few minutes later, Melissa asked, "Is Tavin coming today?"

Grace shrugged, "He was very non-committal, when I talked to him yesterday."

Melissa frowned, "That's odd," she stated.

Nodding, Grace sipped the mimosa. The sweet taste mixed with the fizzing champagne was delicious.

"I know right?" Grace commented.

After their talk of college and Grace's future last week, things changed.

At first, Grace thought she was just being paranoid and "borrowing trouble" but he was distant.

They hadn't spent much time together since then, Tavin explaining that he was training for the rodeo finals.

Even though Grace understood, it still didn't make her feel any more secure about their budding relationship.

"Well," Melissa said, knocking her out of her dark thoughts, "maybe he'll surprise you."

From Melissa's lips to God's ears as far as Grace was concerned. Even so, Grace thought maybe it would take a lot more for Tavin to figure out that their time together wasn't just an affair.

Jutting out her chin, Grace smiled, "Well, it's his loss if he doesn't come today," she raised her glass, "good food and great company."

Melissa smiled and said, "Amen to that!"

They tapped glasses and then the doorbell rang.

"Oh," Melissa said, putting down her glass, "our crowd is starting to arrive."

They walked to the door and found John and several of the ranch hands at the door.

When everyone piled inside, Melissa set them up in the living room with chips and dip and set the television channel to the requested football game.

Within minutes you could hear occasional outbursts followed by the chomp-chomp of chips.

"Takes so little to amuse them," Melissa said sarcastically in the kitchen.

Laughing, Grace shook her head.

The two ladies started getting the green bean casserole going and got the yams on the stove when Raelynn and Seth arrived.

"Greetings," Raelynn announced when she got to the kitchen doorway.

Melissa put down the spoons he was stirring the yams with and walked over to give her friend a hug. "Hello there," She smiled and said, "Happy Thanksgiving."

Raelynn took off her jacket and maneuvered her expanding size onto a chair.

Grace walked over and gave her friend a hug and kiss.

When she pulled away, Grace caught the look in Raelynn's eyes and thought it was a look of pity.

Frowning, she went back to the stove and allowed Melissa and Raelynn to chat.

Since Grace's back was to them, Raelynn nodded toward her and mouthed, "He's not coming."

Sighing, Melissa shook her head. She mouthed in return, "What's his damage?"

Raelynn shrugged.

They started talking about other things but both decided that Tavin McCormick was an ass for not coming.

Tavin adjusted the saddle for his horse and got ready to hop up into the saddle when he heard Rich coming through the barn.

"What are you doing here?" Rich asked.

Shrugging, Tavin put his foot in the stirrup and hoisted himself up into his saddle. He adjusted the reins and turned the horse to head out into the pasture.

Rich called after him, "You know, you can't run!"

Waving absently, Tavin kept going.

He was well out onto the ranch land when he pulled his horse up. Rich was right, of course, but Tavin wasn't ready to admit it.

After the night in front of the fire when Grace said he made her happy, he just shut down. It felt like now there was some damn expectation and he couldn't handle that.

She called him yesterday and asked him to come today and he hemmed and hawed about something but never really said whether he would go.

When Seth called him this morning, probably because his wife asked him to, and asked him to come he almost said yes.

Maybe he couldn't run indefinitely but, for now, that was what he needed to do.

The meal was delicious. Melissa and Grace received praise from all the guys and Raelynn. All the traditional things were there, along with a few new things.

Everyone ate until the women shooed them back to the living room for more football.

The three women stayed in the kitchen and cleaned up the mess, preparing plates for each of the guys to take with them back to the ranch.

"Thank you both again," Raelynn said as she put saran wrap over plates.

Grace smiled and kept washing the dishes in the sink.

Melissa put away a container and answered, "You are more than welcome," she winked at her friend and added, "next year is on you!"

Raelynn laughed, "You got it!"

After everything was cleaned up, the women got out the pumpkin and apple pies they made. Orders were taken and dessert was served to the guys with specific orders about not getting food on the furniture. Everyone talked about football and commented on the cooking. Stories of past Thanksgivings were thrown into the mix.

It was dark when everyone left. John stayed so he could spend time with Melissa which meant Grace was left to her own devices.

She went up to her room and called her parents' home to wish them Happy Thanksgiving. Her brother was there so she spoke to him too. Hearing their voices made her a little homesick but she was glad that their day was good.

Messaging Hailey on FB, she closed her laptop and turned on the television.

The only thing that could've made the day better was if Tavin was there.

Tavin rode into the barn and got off his horse. He was brushing down the animal when he heard a noise behind him.

It was Seth.

"Howdy," He said to his friend.

Seth smiled and handed Tavin a plate, "Here's what you missed," he said and started to walk away.

Puzzled, Tavin stared after him until he was in his truck and pulling out. What the hell was that about?

Tavin set the plate aside so he could finish getting his horse settled, then he took it into the house.

Putting the plate into the microwave, he heated it up for a minute, then took it out.

Even being leftovers, the food smelled heavenly.

He sat down at the table and ate the food. It was awesome!

The food was gone and he wondered how he ate it all so fast. 'Because it was good, stupid.' He said to himself.

Going upstairs, Tavin showered and changed into a clean pair of jeans and sweater.

Without thinking too much, he went out and started up his truck.

Before he could come up with some cockamamie reason to stay away from Grace, he pulled out of his driveway and headed to her house.

Grace was starting to nod off to a movie when she heard her aunt call out, "Grace, honey, can you come downstairs?"

Rubbing the sleep from her eyes, Grace got up and opened the door. She could here John talking. When she was halfway down the stairs, she could see who John was talking to.......it was Tavin!

Tavin turned to see Grace on the stairs and his breath caught in his chest.

"Happy Thanksgiving," He said softly.

Grace looked from Tavin, to John, then to her aunt. What was going on?

Knowing Grace was unsure about what to do, Melissa spoke up, "John, let's go watch a movie in my room?"

John, clearly not sure what was going on, answered, "Uh, sure."

They left the room but neither Tavin nor Grace moved from where they were.

Finally, Tavin broke the silence by saying, "The customary response when someone says "Happy Thanksgiving" is to say it back."

Still unable to speak, Grace was glued to the spot on the stairs.

Tavin realized he was in trouble. She was probably mad that he didn't come earlier and he needed to find a way to apologize.

He was at the base of the stairs when Grace put up her hands, "You know," she began, "just when I think you'll be okay with our relationship, you pull something that makes me doubt it."

In an attempt to divert attention, Tavin asked, "How do you see our "relationship"?"

Grace shook her head, "It doesn't seem to matter how I see it Tavin, it matters that you don't."

Her words hurt, as he was sure they were meant to. She was hurting because he couldn't handle being close.

He stood there, at the bottom of the stairs, and looked up at her.

She was beautiful! Her hair was mussed, probably from napping, and her cheeks were flushed. She wore a blue sweater that looked soft. It was fitted enough to show off her curves and made him ache to touch her.

Knowing he was asking for it, he asked, "Don't what, Grace?"

Grace shook her head back and forth in frustration, "Don't seem to think that we actually have a relationship," she answered flatly.

He was going to answer but her look silenced him.

"Despite what you apparently think," Grace said, her voice hitching, "I'm not a child."

Tavin's smile faded, "I don't think of you that way."

Grace rebutted, "But you don't think that dating someone requires respect."

His shackles being raised, Tavin clenched his jaw. "Have I disrespected you?" He asked.

She nodded, "I think so Tavin." Finally coming down the steps, she stopped at the bottom one, bringing her face to face with him. "I think you want someone to sleep with and," she waved her hands, "they get the least bit close, you push them away."

He knew she was right. That didn't make it any easier for him to admit it out loud.

Grace stood there and watched him. Normally she wouldn't let him stand there and stew, but she was tired. Tired of trying to fall in love with someone who clearly had no intention of responding in kind.

"You may be right," Tavin said, "but I'm here now."

Oh, she wished it was that simple. She wished she could sweep away the doubts, but now, she was knee deep in them and didn't want to put any more effort into someone who wasn't willing.

"Maybe," Grace answered in a defeated voice, "you'll figure out what I'm talking about."

Grace felt exhausted, physically and emotionally, and turned to go back upstairs.

She was halfway up when she turned around and said, "Happy Thanksgiving Tavin."

Standing at the bottom of the stairs in Melissa's house. Tavin figured out he just made the biggest mistake ever but had absolutely no idea how to fix it.

He couldn't just stand there, so Tavin sighed and left.

Grace stood at the top of the stairs and waited to hear the click of the front door closing before she sank to the floor and cried.

Chapter 21

Two weeks later, Grace got up out of bed and sighed heavily. She did it every day now, as if the process of simply getting out of bed were draining her of all energy.

She got ready for work and went downstairs to find Melissa standing in the kitchen, a cup of coffee in her hand, and the other hand on her hip.

"It's time for an intervention," Melissa announced.

Grace groaned inwardly. She was not up to this right now.

Smiling, Grace walked over and got out a box of cereal from the cupboard, poured some in a bowl, got out milk, and poured that in the bowl. When she was at the table, she made a big production of eating. She was silently saying, "I'm fine."

Melissa watched her niece and knew it was a façade. She wasn't born yesterday and didn't buy into the "it's okay," crap Grace proceeded to use.

She even called her sister the night before, hoping for some awesome insight she may not have. Her sister was worried but told Melissa that "part of letting your children grow up was letting them find their own solutions to problems."

When she hung up, she was more upset than before she called. 'Damn Tavin McCormick' she repeated to herself again. He seemed like a nice man but then why was he hurting her niece this way?

Deciding to confront Grace, Melissa walked over and sat across from her.

"Listen up missy," Melissa said in her best motherly voice.

Grace looked up to make eye contact with her aunt, her eyes blank.

Melissa was so upset by the haunted look in her niece's eyes that she had to sit back. She was just this side of tears and hated feeling so helpless.

Clearing her throat, Melissa said, "I'm not the only one who has noticed your moratorium on life."

'This was exhausting,' Grace thought to herself. "I know, I'm trying," She snapped at her aunt.

"That's it," Melissa said, and got up from the table.

Grace knew she upset her aunt but really didn't care at the moment. So she was a little down, who cares! She'd get over it soon enough.

Melissa stomped into her bedroom and picked up the phone. She dialed Raelynn's number and waited for her friend to answer. When she did, Melissa launched into a tirade about Tavin and wanted to know what Raelynn thought.

Blowing out a breath, Raelynn was flabbergasted. She hadn't realized how badly Tavin's rejection affected Grace.

"I'm sorry," She said to Melissa.

Her eyes tearing up, Melissa smiled. Leave it to Raelynn to apologize for something she had no hand in doing.

She said, "Thank you," and asked, "Do I go over there and beat the crap out of him or what?"

"Well," Raelynn answered, "you can try but he's not there, he's at the Rodeo Finals in Las Vegas."

Melissa snorted, "Great, now he leaves us here to clean up his mess."

She heard a noise and turned around in time to see Grace standing in the doorway of her room.

Grace choked out, "You consider me a mess?"

"I'll call you back," Melissa said into the phone and hung it up. She walked over and pulled Grace into her arms, "No sweetie," she crooned, "I'm just so angry at Tavin for hurting you."

Nodding into her aunt's shoulder, Grace said, "I know," through her tears.

Deep down, Grace knew it wasn't entirely Tavin's fault. He did come over and was trying but she shut him down. She just didn't want to hurt anymore.

Sniffling, Melissa smiled and pulled back. "You know what," she said, "we're going riding today."

The look of worry in Grace's eyes was almost her complete undoing. She rubbed her niece's arm and said, "He's out of town."

Grace nodded. Riding did sound fun. Anything that didn't involve thinking too much sounded fun at this point.

Melissa waited for Grace to go upstairs to change and then she called Raelynn back. A plan had to be put in place.

An hour later, they were pulling into the driveway at Seth and Raelynn's place. They could see some of the hands doing things around the main house and barn.

Once they were close enough, Grace saw that they were hanging Christmas lights.

Raelynn met them as they were getting out of the car. Grace noticed her belly was bigger and her waddle much more pronounced.

"Whoa," Melissa said, "how big is this kid gonna be?" She punctuated her words with a Texas twang.

John came out of the barn and stopped behind Melissa, "It's gonna be the biggest pony we've ever seen," he said and smiled when Melissa turned around and kissed him.

"I'd appreciate it," Raelynn said sarcastically, "if everyone would stop referring to my offspring as some sort of farm animal."

They all laughed and Grace felt lighter on the inside. It was good to laugh.

Grace looked over at John and asked, "Do the guys need help?"

John waved his hand, "Naw," he took Melissa's arm and led her toward the barn, "these cowpokes have the Christmas decoratin down now."

His accent and straightforwardness were some of his best traits as far as Grace was concerned. No wonder her aunt adored him.

Grace was a few steps behind her aunt and John when they stopped and turned around.

Pointing to the house, John said, "Now Lynn, you take yourself and that yungin back into the house before Seth has us all strung up for not keepin an eye on you."

Pursing her lips to avoid breaking out in a laugh, Grace couldn't even look at Raelynn. She could hear the woman grumbling and heard the house door slam before she let out a guffaw.

Melissa cleared her throat in an attempt to keep quiet. "John," She said, "you shouldn't talk to her like that."

Nodding, John answered, "Probably not but I'd rather have Miss Lynn riled than have Seth wear out my hide for not keeping a proper eye on her." He tapped Melissa's nose, "And you tearin into my hide for not takin care of your friend."

Knowing he had a point, Melissa chuckled and replied, "You're right about that."

Grace followed them to the barn and chuckled the whole way. She needed this, needed to get out of her comfort zone and realize there was still fun to be had.

Charlie, one of Seth's hands, had their horses saddled and ready to go. He smiled at Grace as he helped her up into the saddle.

"You have a good ride now, Ms. Grace," Charlie said when he had her safely sitting in the saddle.

Smiling down at him, Grace returned, "Thank you Charlie."

The fact that Ms. Grace knew his name made him blush. She was sure a pretty little thing, all the guys noticed her. There was talk that she was seeing Mr. McCormick from the neighboring spread but recent word was that she was now unattached.

Grace led the way as she and Melissa road out from the main ranch area. They followed the path they took the last time they rode.

Once they were a quarter mile from the buildings, Grace gave Cindy the signal to go.

Breaking out into a cantor, Grace allowed the horse to take her wherever the animal wanted. She never even looked behind her to see if her aunt was keeping up.

The wind flew past her, making her hair fly up behind her. The feeling of freedom was so welcomed after these last couple of weeks.

Her aunt was right, she was in some sort of vacation from life.

"No More!" Grace yelled out loud.

After a couple of miles, she slowed Cindy down and walked along a grove of trees. There was a little creek that ran parallel to them. This late in the year, the water was bubbling along, making her think of summer days. 'Too bad it wasn't warm enough to stick her feet in the water,' she wondered as she rode.

Grace reached down and rubbed Cindy's neck, "I know, it sure would be nice to be like that all the time wouldn't it?" She asked the horse.

Cindy's answering nicker made Grace laugh. Apparently the horse understood what she was saying.

There was a bend in the creek that made it turn into the grove of trees.

Some of the leaves were on the ground due to the season but it was still very green. Grace studied the branches of the trees at the side of the creek. They hung over the water as if protecting it.

Grace dismounted and walked slowly, holding Cindy's reins in her hand. If the horse stopped to nibble on some grass, Grace waited.

A while later, they were still walking when Grace heard a horse approaching. The sound of hooves was distinctive.

Looking around, Grace spotted the rider. It was a man. She wondered, if for only a second, whether it was Tavin. As the horse got closer, Grace could see it was Charlie.

As soon as Charlie spotted Grace walking with her horse, he spurred his horse into gear. Once he was close enough, he could see her smiling, and walking without any problems.

"I was wondering if you were okay Ms. Grace," Charlie said when he brought his horse to a halt a few feet from where Grace stood with Cindy.

Smiling, Grace said, "Oh, I'm fine Charlie, we were just walking."

Charlie nodded. "Ms. Melissa came back and asked me to come and fetch you."

Grace frowned and wondered if her aunt was upset.

Seeing Ms. Grace's worry, Charlie spoke up, "She wasn't mad or nothin, she just wanted to make sure you found your way back to the ranch house okay." He kicked a rock with the toe of his boot, "She's inside with Ms. Raelynn."

Nodding, Grace started walking again. Charlie moved up beside her with his horse to keep her company.

"Charlie," Grace said a few minutes later, "how long have you worked for Seth?"

Scratching his chin, Charlie thought about it. "I reckon it's been about five years now," he answered.

Figuring that Charlie wasn't that much older than her, she asked, "Did you go to college?"

Charlie snorted, "No ma'am," he said, "College and me weren't what you'd call compatible."

His answer made Grace laugh. Not at him, at the fact that he seemed to know what was right for him.

She looked over and explained, "I wasn't laughing at you, just interested that you knew it wasn't for you."

Charlie let his mount stop to get a drink from the creek.

He thought about what she said, "It wasn't that I "knew" it," he said slowly, "it was like I knew I didn't want to sit in a classroom for 4 years to figure out life."

That seemed reasonable to Grace.

They walked for a while longer and finally decided they needed to get back before Melissa or John sent out the cavalry.

The ride back was easy, they kept up a good pace and even raced for part of the way. Grace was pretty sure Charlie let her win but she'd take it anyway.

After they got back to the barn, Charlie helped her down off of Cindy.

"I'll get the horses settled in," Charlie said as they walked into the barn.

Grace was touched by his sweetness, "Thank you," she said and leaned over to kiss his cheek. It was an impulsive move but she was feeling so much lighter emotionally.

Charlie blushed, "I'll be free to take a ride tomorrow if you like," he said before leading the horses away.

She walked up to the main house and thought that maybe she needed to be out and with new people and that would help her get over Tavin and their disastrous whatever it was.

Grace knocked and entered the back door, per Raelynn's previous instructions.

She walked through the kitchen and into the great room. The layout here was very similar to the way Tavin's house was set up.

'Get him out of your head,' she told herself.

When she entered, she saw Raelynn and Melissa on the sofa. The women smiled when they saw her.

"Hey," Melissa said, noticing the new flush in her niece's cheeks, she smiled.

Grace answered, "Hey," and sat down on a chair facing them.

Raelynn asked, "How was your ride?"

Smiling, Grace answered, "Great!"

Relief flooded Melissa's heart. Grace looked better, like she was pulled out of the funk she was in.

"You left me in the dust," Melissa said teasingly.

Nodding, Grace reached over and stole her aunt's glass of water and took a drink.

The women laughed and continued their talk.

Chapter 22

A week later, Grace woke up feeling light hearted. Every day she went into the office and left a little early so she could go to Seth and Raelynn's for a ride. Cindy was quickly becoming her new best friend.

The horse whinnied whenever Grace walked into the barn. They were becoming in tune with each other and mostly just walked.

A couple of times, Charlie rode with her. He was always very polite and kept his distance physically. Grace figured he probably thought she was still dating Tavin or something.

Most of the guys she knew would have at least tried to kiss her by now but Charlie was the epitome of a gentleman. Seeing him made Grace realize what her Aunt Melissa saw in John.

A week after their first ride, she was waiting on Charlie when she heard some of the other hands yelling. Curious about what was happening, she followed the noise into an office at the end of the barn.

She stood in the doorway of the office and could see the guys all gathered around a television. They were quiet for a minute, then would erupt into yelling.

One of the guys spotted her and slapped another on the shoulder, "Psst, we have company," he said.

"Oh Ms. Grace," Another one of the hands said, "Sorry if we were disturbing you."

Grace looked at all of them and smiled, "You weren't," she said, "I was just wondering what all the excitement was about."

Charlie came up behind her, "They're watching the rodeo finals," he said.

"Oh," Grace answered and walked away.

She had no business seeing what was going on with all of that. It wasn't like she had anyone she was rooting for anymore.

Charlie caught up to her outside the barn and touched her arm gently. He asked, "Are you okay?"

Smiling, Grace answered, "Oh yes."

They went out and got up into the saddles of their respective horses and set out past the buildings.

Even with Cindy's happy whinnies, Grace was distracted.

After only a few minutes, she saw Charlie turn his horse around.

She frowned and asked, "Is everything alright?"

"Ms. Grace," Charlie began, "I'm a cowboy so I live a pretty simple life." He pulled his horse up to stop so he could look at her, "And I realize when someone isn't telling the truth to me, or themselves."

After a week, she thought she was doing a pretty good job at covering up her hurt. Apparently she was wrong.

Smiling, she looked at Charlie, "You realize don't you, that you are a genius?" She asked him.

Charlie blushed, "No ma'am," he said, "just seeing that I don't stand a chance with the prettiest lady I've ever met."

Now Grace blushed, "Oh Charlie," Grace winked, "if you're referring to me, I'm not the prettiest lady," she took his hand in hers, "just the luckiest one for having you for a friend."

"Yeah, yeah," Charlie groaned, "another 'Sorry Charlie,' for me."

Grace laughed. "And did I mention sweet and funny?" She asked.

She had such a knack for making him blush and Charlie really enjoyed spending time with her. He couldn't say he wasn't disappointed in the fact that she wasn't sweet on him in return, but he was a big boy and could handle himself.

Releasing his hand, Grace pulled her reins to head for the ranch.

The next evening, Grace was exhausted. She put her first full day in at Melissa's office and was stiff from sitting at the desk all day.

It was good to get back into the swing of things but work was just that, work!

She came down to find John and Melissa in the living room. John was yelling at the tv like the ranch hands were at the ranch the day before.

Sighing, Grace walked in and sat down in a chair.

John looked at Melissa, silently asking if they should change the channel.

"Are you okay to watch this?" Melissa asked her niece. "If not, we can go in my room."

Grace shook her head no, "I'm fine," she answered and settled back into the chair to watch.

The bull riders were on and Grace winced every time one of them came out on the huge animals. They were so small, comparatively speaking, and looked like rag dolls being tossed around by the huge bulls.

A commercial came on and Grace let out the breath she didn't realize she was holding. 'Holy Cow!' She thought to herself, 'How do they do that?'

Looking over, she saw John writing something on a piece of paper and Melissa smiling at him. She looked up at Grace and rolled her eyes, which made Grace laugh.

"What?" John said when he looked up to see his girlfriend and her niece exchanging glances.

Grace frowned and answered, "Nothing," in a tight voice.

John was smart enough to know that when a woman said "nothing" it was the opposite of what she meant but he didn't want to borrow trouble so he went back to writing notes to give to Rich.

"He takes notes and lets Rich know some statistics and comments about the riders for when he and Tavin train." Melissa volunteered.

'Ahhh,' Grace thought to herself, then asked, "I thought Tavin did the bronc riding not bull riding?"

Now John piped up, "Rich trains other riders as well and some of them ride bulls."

Sitting back, Grace felt silly that she didn't know that and just answered, "Oh."

The three of them watched as the Bronc Riding event was announced, then a commercial came on the television.

Melissa stood up, and said, "Grace, you don't have to watch this you know."

"I know," Grace answered and smiled, "but I'd like to."

John watched the interplay between the women and was swearing a blue streak on the inside. He'd tear that boy a new one when he got the chance.

Grace walked into the kitchen and got a bottled water. She went back into the living room and sat down in the chair. Taking a deep breath, she leaned back and waited.

The announcer came back on the screen and announced the Bronc Riding event. She didn't know the names of the first few riders introduced so she studied their performances the way she might study a ballet dancer's movements.

It amazed Grace that the event only lasted 8 seconds. That's all the time the rider had to stay on. Of course, if you took into account that these horses were a good part of a ton of muscle and they really didn't want you on their backs, well, that made things a lot more interesting.

John would comment here and there but Grace only half listened. She waited anxiously, wanting to see Tavin ride.

Finally, the announcer said Tavin's name. Grace leaned forward in the chair hoping to catch every detail. The cameras were hopping from view to view.

First, they shot him in the stall with the bronc. Then, they spanned back from, what looked like, across the arena.

Without a lot of notice, he was shot out of the pen. The horse immediately started bucking and was actually airborne. Tavin's arm held fast as his body and legs seemed to move with the animals contorted positions.

It seemed to be a lot of anticipation on the rider's part and a heck of a lot of meanness on the horse's.

The buzzer went off, which meant that Tavin had completed the ride. They only had to wait for his scores.

'Thank goodness he wasn't hurt,' Grace said to herself.

She looked over at John, who had a big smile on his face. Grace smiled until she saw John's face turn into a frown.

When she turned around she saw Tavin pinned between the bronc and the railing. The horse was still moving and seemed to be slamming Tavin against the fence.

"Dear Lord," Grace yelled and stood up.

Tavin was feeling good. His hand felt secure and he nodded to his team. Within a second or so, the chute swung open and he was off on his ride.

He "marked out" as soon as the animal was free, making sure his points were good.

This bronc was a good one, known as Devil's Pride, and he was living up to his name.

Alternating his upper body with his legs, Tavin felt the way the bronc was going and moved with the animal as best he could.

The buzzer sounded and he was still on, hopefully with a good score.

Smiling, he made eye contact with one of the pick-up men used to help him get off the bronc after the event. The guy was nodding and looking at the bronc but didn't anticipate the animal's sharp turn.

Trying to get his hand loose from the lead rope, Tavin saw the fence coming close and tried to get free but his glove, somehow, got caught. He was thrown off the side of the horse and was wedged between the animal and the fence.

He felt the wood slam into his side as the bronc bucked over and over again.

The pick-up men managed to get the horse away from him after, what felt like forever. Someone got his glove loose and he could feel the air of the arena rush into his lungs. He hadn't realized before that the horse's weight wasn't allowing him to breathe.

Pain shot through his chest and he bent over, trying to catch his breath.

The crowd was making noises, not sure if he was okay or not. He waved and motioned for one of the guys to help him out of the arena.

"Is he okay?" Grace demanded of John.

He couldn't lie to her and answered, "Anytime a rider is walking out, it's a good sign."

His answer did not reassure Grace. She started pacing the living room, waiting for the announcer to say something about Tavin's condition.

The score for his ride was posted and John whooped behind her.

Grace's glare was hot and intense. How could he be glad when Tavin was hurt? She couldn't understand men and their need to put themselves in harm's way.

Melissa saw her niece and hurt for her. She'd seen enough of these rodeos to be fairly certain Tavin was okay, but she didn't want to speak too soon, just in case.

The announcer came on and said, "We just heard that Tavin McCormick is okay," he clapped, "he is being taken to the hospital to be checked out but he is walking and is awake."

"Good news," John said.

Grace sighed but wasn't completely convinced.

She watched John sit down and wait to watch more of this but she just couldn't.

"I'm going up to bed," Grace said to her aunt.

Melissa nodded, "Okay sweetie, sleep well."

The words were meant to comfort Grace, but they both knew she wouldn't sleep well.

The next morning, Grace got up and went downstairs. She found her aunt sitting in the kitchen, her steaming cup of coffee in front of her.

Looking expectantly, Grace asked, "Any news?"

It was apparent her niece was still very worried about Mr. McCormick. Of course, Melissa just wanted to punch him for the pain he'd caused her niece. Instead she sighed.

"A couple of broken ribs and a bruised back," Melissa said calmly.

Grace sighed. It wasn't great but it wasn't anything life threatening.

The next logical question popped into Grace's mind.

She asked Melissa, "When will he be home?"

Smiling, Melissa knew Grace would ask so she made sure to find out as much as possible from Rich and John.

"They said he'll be home this afternoon," Melissa said.

Nodding, Grace went to the refrigerator and got out the juice to pour herself a glass. Before she could, she stood at the counter and looked at her aunt.

Looking at her hands, which were now clenched in front of her, Grace inquired, "You think I shouldn't care right?"

Getting up, Melissa walked over and folded Grace into her arms.

She murmured, "No," into Grace's hair. "I would be disappointed if you didn't care."

The statement threw Grace, she looked up at her aunt, puzzled.

Melissa went back over and sat down at the table. She cupped the coffee cup between her hands.

"I spoke to John last night after you went up," Melissa started, "and he said that Tavin cares for you."

The news didn't sit well with Grace, "He has a very odd way of showing it," she replied sarcastically.

She couldn't help it, Melissa smiled. Her niece was just like her, stubborn.

Leaning forward, Melissa added, "He does," she sighed before saying, "he just puts up these obstacles like your age difference, your education, and he doesn't know how to accept that you love him."

Grace didn't need her aunt to be quite that honest. Looking skeptical, she shook her head no.

"Yes," Melissa said, disputing her niece's denial.

Walking over, Grace sat down at the table across from her aunt. This whole thing was confusing the crap out of her.

Sighing, Grace said, "Well, I don't want to love him."

Melissa couldn't help it, she laughed.

"It's not funny," Grace said with a clenched jaw.

Nodding, Melissa placed her hand over Grace's and spoke softly, "You are so much like me. We want what we want, when we want, and when someone doesn't do what we want, it's a mess and we don't want it at all."

"Okay," Grace said, "that didn't clear anything up."

Chuckling, Melissa said, "You may not want to love him sweetie, but you do."

Grumbling to herself, Grace wondered if she could find a hole nearby and stick her head in it.

Chapter 23

Tavin walked into the house and slowly lowered himself onto the couch. Rich walked in behind him and took his bags upstairs.

Listening to the sound of his luggage being tossed onto the floor, Tavin grinned. Rich was like John, they were old-time cowboys who didn't take anyone's shit.

He heard his friend clomp back down the stairs and laid there, his eyes closed, waiting for Rich to say something.

"Heard from John this morning," Rich began. "Said that Grace was real worried about you when she saw your screw up with that bronc."

Leave it to Rich to blame him for something that was just a twist of fate. Nodding, Tavin opened one eye enough to see his friend standing at the back of the couch and glaring down at him.

Tavin closed his eye again and asked his friend, "Is there something you need?"

The reasonable part of Tavin's brain knew he should take the pain medication the ER doctor prescribed for him but the cowboy in him wanted to just deal with it.

In its own way, the pain made him realize he was still here. Plus it kept him from thinking about Grace.

"Damn fool," Rich spat out as he walked into the kitchen.

Tavin couldn't help but think that Rich was certainly the smarter of the two of them at this moment.

Grace went to work, thankful that it was Friday. She wanted to just get through the day so she could call John to see if he knew how Tavin was doing.

She told herself that she wasn't going to go out there to see him…. no matter what!

As much as she worried and as much as her aunt may say the "L" word was involved, Grace couldn't swallow her pride and go to him.

Well into a complex file, her aunt wanted tediously examined, Grace didn't hear anyone else come in the office.

She happened to look up when she reached for her bottled water and jumped at the sight of Brandon only a foot or two in front of the desk.

Her hand flew to her throat, trying to calm her body down from the scare.

"Brandon," Grace said sharply, "what are you doing in here?"

He just stood there, looking at her.

The intensity of his stare was starting to make her feel really uncomfortable when her aunt came into the room.

Grace could see Melissa understood the situation immediately and was spurred into action.

"Brandon," Melissa said sternly, "the fact that you have a crush on my niece is sweet," she placed her hand on his shoulder, "but the fact that you're creeping her out isn't."

Melissa walked over so she was standing between Grace and the boy.

"So, you have the choice of resigning and finding another internship or….." Melissa paused for a moment, then added, "nothing, you are fired."

Grace wanted to laugh at Brandon's shocked expression. Luckily, he must have had a flash of decency because he nodded and turned to walk out of the office.

Turning to face her niece, Melissa was relieved.

"Thank goodness," She said and smiled at Grace.

Without the looming Brandon to make her feel weird, Grace dove into the files and finished with a smile on her face.

As soon as she was in the car with her aunt, she dialed John's number.

"This is John," He answered.

Grace smiled, "John, it's Grace," she started and then looked over to see her aunt smiling at her, "I was wondering if you'd talked to Rich today?"

John pointed to the far side of the corral to instruct the guys on where they needed to be. Once they were moving around to their places, he turned his attention back to the phone.

He spoke up to be heard over the noise of the animals, "Talked to him earlier, TJ is home resting," John chuckled then added, "I guess the boy is pretty banged up."

Hearing the words made Grace upset. Why did men think it was funny when another man was hurt? She would probably never figure out the way their minds worked. Actually, she really didn't want to know how their minds worked.

"Well," Grace said, frowning, "thanks."

John figured she was going to hang up and he felt obliged to be honest with the young un. "Grace," He said loudly, "I heard from Rich that Tavin was asking about you."

Nodding, Grace said, "Thanks," again and hung up the phone.

Melissa waited for her niece to hang up before asking, "How's he doing?"

"I guess, he's banged up but fine," Grace said on a sigh.

Melissa watched her niece and felt sorry for her. It was times like these when she was grateful for hers and John's relationship. They were straightforward in their wants and needs and nobody was playing games.

After pulling into the driveway and shutting off the car, Melissa turned to face Grace.

"You know," Melissa said to her niece, "nobody would think you were being silly if you just went out there."

Grace knew her aunt was right and nodded. It wasn't that easy though.

Opening the car door, Grace said, "It wouldn't be so bad if he didn't shut me down at every turn."

Her niece was right, Melissa agreed with her about Tavin's behavior but still, she was in love with him and love meant bending one's will and putting aside one's pride sometimes.

They opened the door and went inside. Melissa went into the kitchen to check the roast she put in the crock pot this morning. The smell of the meat was tangy and made her mouth water.

She turned around to find Grace wasn't behind her. Smiling, Melissa turned the roast and wondered how long it would take Grace to get out the door and into the car.

Upstairs, Grace was sitting on her bed brooding. 'It isn't fair,' she said to herself.

Taking off her clothes, she pulled out a t-shirt and jeans. Yanking on the top, Grace looked in the mirror and saw a sad person.

"Damn it Tavin," She called out in exasperation and grabbed her purse.

Twenty minutes later she was tearing down his driveway and cursing herself the whole way. This was really very absurd. He probably didn't even want to see her and she was putting herself out there…..again….to be kicked in the proverbial teeth. Fantastic!

She stopped the car in front of the main house. There were people moving around the other buildings and she really didn't want an audience if the conversation between her and Tavin didn't go well.

After getting out of her car, Grace absently smoothed down her t-shirt and walked around the vehicle to the front porch steps.

Each step felt like a chipping at her resolve. She knew this wasn't the best idea. So why was she here? "Because," she said out loud, "you're a doormat!"

Hearing herself say the words, Grace grimaced.

Tavin was on the couch, flipping through channels on the television and trying not to go insane when there was a knock on the door.

He couldn't move well enough without feeling like a heard of stallions was stampeding across his chest, so he yelled out, "Come on in."

Grace entered the house slowly. She didn't know who would be here and didn't really know what she was going to say to Tavin anyway.

"Hello?" Tavin called, "I can't move to see anything so you'll have to come over here."

This was one of those moments when an idea, that you would normally not have, pops into your mind. Grace didn't have these mental hiccups often but she was having a helluva doozy right now.

Laying there, Tavin wondered if maybe his mind was playing tricks on him. He thought he heard a knock but maybe not since no one was answering.

"Hello?" He asked again.

Did he take the medication the doctor prescribed? He wasn't sure. Trying to turn enough to get a look behind him, he grimaced in pain.

Grace watched him from behind and felt awful when he was trying to move and hissed with the discomfort.

Quietly, she slipped off her shoes and undid the button of her jeans.

A few feet into the room, she pulled the t-shirt over her head and let it fall silently on a nearby chair.

Tavin closed his eyes, thinking he was going nuts. Just as well, the sleep would help him let go of the pain.

In just her bra and panties, Grace softly padded around the couch. He was laying there, his eyes closed. 'Yay,' Grace said to herself.

Once she was around the piece of furniture and standing in front of him she mussed up her hair and popped her hip out to one side, trying to give him a sexy pose.

"Mmmhmmm," Grace made the noise.

Tavin's eyes opened in time to see an almost naked Grace standing 2 feet in front of him. The shock of seeing her along with the knowledge of what that body did to his, took him into the world of arousal in no time flat.

Without thinking, he tried to sit up. The pain of the movement was horrific and he yelled out in agony.

Grace cringed at the sound he made and felt awful. She was about to step forward to help him when a concerned Rich came out of another doorway off the room.

"Uh," Rich said before looking away, "hello Grace."

'Oh Lord,' Grace said as she died inside of humiliation.

Tavin was doubled over in pain and Rich was standing a few feet away trying not to look at her mostly naked body.

Not knowing what to do, Grace ran around the couch and grabbed her clothes. She pulled the t-shirt over her head raggedly and had her jeans pulled up over her hips before she was at the door.

By this time, Rich was smiling like a little boy who got his first look at a girl and Tavin was still gripping the couch in obvious discomfort.

"I'm sorry," Grace yelled before running out the door and down the steps.

She was in her car and peeling out of the driveway in no time flat.

Rich stood in the living room staring at Tavin.

"I suppose she wouldn't consider doing that on a regular basis huh?" Rich asked.

Picking up a nearby magazine, Tavin threw it at Rich.

'Poor Grace,' he thought. She was probably halfway to Lake Jackson by now.

Shaking his head, because that was the only part of him he could move without pain, Tavin laid back against the couch and wondered how they would ever talk again.

Chapter 24

Two days later, Melissa, Grace, and John were sitting down to Sunday dinner.

Grace hadn't mentioned the humiliating encounter with Tavin and Rich. Her aunt asked if she saw Tavin and she was honest and said, "yes," but didn't offer up any other details.

She honestly did not know what she would say to either of the men IF she ever saw them again.

They were leisurely discussing the upcoming Christmas celebrations when John turned to Grace.

"I heard you started giving shows now," He said and bit his lip.

Melissa was lost and looked at Grace with questioning eyes.

Grace's cheeks turned bright red, Oh Lord, he heard about her oops.

Trying to remain calm, Grace smiled sweetly and said, "No, it was a simple misunderstanding."

John shook his head, "I heard that you were giving a performance and Rich, from how he told it to me, really enjoyed it."

If there was a possibility that the ground could open up and swallow her whole, she wished it would happen now.

"What do you mean?" Melissa asked, looking back and forth between John and Grace.

Feeling flushed, Grace cleared her throat and mumbled, "I wanted to "surprise" Tavin and was not dressed appropriately when Rich walked into the room."

It took about a minute for Melissa to digest the words. Grace knew when she did because her face contorted in her efforts to avoid laughing.

"Go ahead," Grace challenged, "get it out."

Even John couldn't hold back now, his shoulders were shaking with laughter.

Rolling her eyes, Grace sat there and took the punishment of being embarrassed. She would NEVER do such a stupid thing again.

A week later, Grace was asked by Melissa to go over and give Raelynn a hand with some Christmas party preparations at the ranch.

Every year Seth threw a big party for all the hands and their families, along with some friends. The party grew over the years so that it was now one of the biggest social events of the season.

Now with Raelynn being almost eight months pregnant, she couldn't do everything that needed to be done.

Grace knew her project at the office was almost completed so she jumped at the chance to prolong her reasons for staying here in Texas.

She knew it was silly but it was all she had at the moment.

Since the blow up with Tavin at Thanksgiving, she was thinking long and hard about what she wanted. Taking Tavin out of the equation, she found she still liked being here in Texas, with her aunt, and around the people who cared.

It wasn't that her friends or her brother or her parents didn't care. It was more like, her life there seemed to be more about marking time rather than actually living.

Here, with the horses and the people, she felt content. That was a new sensation for Grace and she recognized that some people never found that in their life. Would she be gypping herself if she ran away again because Tavin hurt her?

The only answer she could come up with was a resounding yes.

Grace drove over to Seth and Grace's ranch mid-morning. The weather was mild but the clouds were moving in.

She was pulling into the driveway when the first plop of rain hit her windshield.

"Oh great," Grace mumbled and tried to get up to the house before the downpour came.

She managed to park and run up onto the porch before the rain came down hard. Sheets of rain slammed into the ground. The water hit so hard that each drop created a tuft of dust where it connected with the dirt.

The front door opened and Raelynn stood in the threshold.

"Come in before you get drenched," She said to Grace.

They walked inside and Grace set her purse on the side table in the entryway.

Once inside the great room, Grace looked around and was, once again, impressed with the size of the room combined with its coziness.

Raelynn did a fantastic job of making it feel welcoming but still rustic. Not an easy task with cowboys running around all the time.

Sitting on the sofa, Grace smiled as Raelynn handed her a glass of tea.

"You don't need to get me anything," Grace said, "I'm here to help you."

Waving her hand in dismissal, Raelynn waddled over to the overstuffed chair across from Grace and sat down as gracefully as her flowering body would allow.

"It's fine," Raelynn sighed as she finally settled.

Grace shook her head in exasperation. Melissa would never forgive her if she didn't help Raelynn with the party planning and anything else that needed doing.

Raelynn pulled out a notebook and handed it to Grace.

Rubbing her extended belly, Raelynn chuckled, "Just a few things left to do."

Looking at the list, Grace was sure her friend was being sarcastic. When she looked up, her thoughts were confirmed.

Raelynn wanted to laugh at the look of fear that crossed Grace's face. Being older and pretty organized herself, Seth's holiday party even threw her for a loop. She could only imagine how Grace was looking at the "to do" list.

"It's okay," Raelynn offered, "I'll help you through it."

Grace nodded, "I sure hope so," she answered.

Three hours later, the two women had half of the list crossed off. There was still a ton of things to do but Grace offered to make some lunch for Raelynn so they could take a break.

Raelynn walked behind her into the kitchen and sat at the table.

"You know," Raelynn said, "I don't remember being this exhausted with Hailey."

Nodding, Grace pulled out the fixings for sandwiches from the refrigerator and pantry. She didn't have anything to contribute since she'd never been pregnant.

Up until now, Grace couldn't remember ever being interested in the condition. She assumed that she would marry and have kids but it was in some faraway place in the back of her mind.

Setting the lunch stuff on the table, Grace asked, "How does it feel being pregnant?"

A knowing smile spread across Raelynn's face and she responded, "I'm not sure it's the same for everyone, but knowing I have part of Seth growing inside me makes me feel very loved," she sighed, "like there's something bigger than the both of us."

Again, Grace nodded. The dreamy look on Raelynn's face made her look almost angelic. Grace hoped she herself could look that way someday.

They ate lunch and sat back down in the great room to finish off more of the dreaded "list."

It was after four in the afternoon when Raelynn announced, "I'm pooped," she struggled to get up out of the chair, "I think I'm going to lay down."

Grace jumped up and helped her get out of the chair and toward the bathroom.

"Can we get together tomorrow morning?" Raelynn asked her as she waddled down the hallway.

Smiling, Grace answered, "Oh sure."

They got to the doorway of the guest bedroom that Raelynn used for daytime naps so she didn't have to walk up the stairs. Raelynn turned and hugged Grace.

Pulling back a little, Raelynn said, "I'm so glad you're here, it makes your aunt so happy."

Grace nodded, "Me too," she said back.

"I miss Hailey," Raelynn said as she walked into the bedroom. "Oh," She turned to face Grace, "can I trouble you to go out to the barn and let Seth know I'm lying down? If I don't answer the phone he goes to Defcon 1."

Chuckling, Grace nodded and said, "Sure."

She walked out of the house smiling.

Tavin was standing in Seth's barn talking to John. He'd come over a few hours earlier to talk about the

NRF ride. Today was the first day he didn't feel like a semi-truck hit him a few times.

"It was a good ride," Tavin said defensively.

John nodded, "Yeah, until you got distracted and let that bronc pin you against the fence."

There was no pleasing John or Rich as far as Tavin was concerned.

He followed John through the barn as he looked over the horses.

"It was a fool thing to do TJ," John commented as she looked over a mare he was thinking of having impregnated in the springtime.

Tavin was relieved that John used his nickname, it meant he wasn't too mad at him for his mistake. He nodded but was silent.

John stopped and turned around to face TJ, "It's because you were distracted with Grace wasn't it?"

No way was he stepping into that quicksand, "NO!" he said loudly.

Tilting his head, John frowned, "Yeah right, and I'm George Strait singin a ballad on horseback," he said sarcastically.

It really irritated Tavin that John, and Rich for that matter, felt they had the right to comment on his love life. Or lack thereof.

"Okay," Tavin yelled, "I'm sick and tired of you and Rich telling me that I am pining for Grace or that I'm thinking about her."

John stood there stone-faced. He wanted to tear the boy a new attitude but, seeing Grace walk into the barn, thought he'd let her do it for him.

Tavin had enough of this crap, his anger rising, he shouted, "I don't "love" her, I wasn't "thinking" about her, and I don't "need" her."

Grace walked into the barn and smiled when she saw John. He was talking to someone but Grace didn't see who it was until she was well down the aisle of stalls. He saw her, she could tell, but stood there and listened to Tavin as he yelled.

"Well," John said tightly and pointed behind Tavin, "Now she knows it."

Tavin closed his eyes. Why did she have to walk into the barn right now? What was she doing here?

He turned around in time to see Grace's look of hurt slide across her face and be covered up by a look of disdain. 'Damn it!' He thought.

John walked around Tavin and over to Grace. He knew what TJ was going to say and didn't stop it. It was better that Grace know the truth of the man she thought was the one she loved. He would never say such things but he was raised to be a gentleman.

Without speaking, John put his arm around Grace and steered her back out of the barn.

"Hello Grace," John said softly, "did you need something?"

Her insides were in her feet but Grace kept enough of her brain engaged to answer, "Raelynn wanted me to let Seth know she was napping."

John nodded and smiled.

They were just outside the barn door, Grace passing on the message from Raelynn, when Tavin appeared.

Grace wanted to run but that wasn't the right thing to do. She wasn't ever for someone running from the problem. In her opinion, that's what Tavin did, not her.

Tavin looked directly at John and asked, "May I speak to Grace alone?"

Looking at Grace, John waited to see what her answer would be. He felt protective of her but knew she was a grown woman who made her own decisions. She nodded at him so he nodded to Tavin and started walking toward the small tool shed.

Before he was out of earshot, John said, "You hurt her again boy, you'll be answerin to me."

Nodding, Tavin knew John meant what he said.

When John was out of sight, Tavin took a step closer to Grace and stopped.

Just looking at him made Grace angry. She wasn't sure why. Maybe it was because he was a coward in her eyes. He told everyone else, practically shouted it from the rooftops, how much he didn't feel for her but his eyes said something else.

"You're a hypocrite," Grace said through gritted teeth.

Standing his ground, Tavin asked, "Me?" He looked around and laughed sarcastically, "How about you?"

Grace never would have believed she could be as enraged as she was right now, how dare he say that to her!

She stalked over to where he stood and got in his face.

"I'm not the one who keeps saying, No, I don't, and then looks at me like that!" Grace yelled at him.

Pride was now building up in his chest, "You're too young," Tavin shouted.

Shaking her head, Grace screamed back, "But that didn't stop you from sleeping with me....... repeatedly!"

It didn't matter that she was right, it only mattered that he won the argument. Even if it meant he was going to hell.

Grace stomped away from him and back into the barn. She needed to get away from him. He was being an ass and she didn't know why. All his arguments, such as they were, truly were ridiculous. It was all his fears and she didn't want to pay the price for him being afraid.

He followed Grace into the barn and stood a few feet away from her. She was leaning on a stall door, looking inside at the horse. Her shoulders were slumped and he knew he hurt her.

"You know what," Grace said and turned to him, "you're right."

She walked over and stood in front of him. Lifting her hand, Grace cupped his cheek. Even though this was over, she wouldn't be the one to throw it away. If he wanted out, it would be on him.

Looking down and then up into his eyes, Grace whispered, "I understand."

She kissed him then, a soft kiss. A goodbye kiss.

When she pulled away she walked around him and out of the barn.

Chapter 25

Tavin stood there, in the center aisle of the barn, and didn't know what to do.

All of a sudden, everything that he did, everything that he wanted to do, didn't mean anything. Before he could over think it, he turned around and started to run after Grace.

Grace was around the front of the house and just opened her car door when she heard Tavin yell her name.

He ran up to her and stopped a few feet away. If he got any closer, he would pull her to him and he needed to get it all out.

They stood there, looking at one another, Grace crying, and Tavin frowning.

It started raining, the sky opening up as it did earlier, with sheets of water pouring over them.

Grace waited and, when he still said nothing, got angry again.

"What the hell is wrong with you?" She screamed at him. "You have no concept of what love is do you?"

Anger coursed through his system and he spouted back, "At least I don't go around sleeping with men and then ignoring them."

It would have hurt more if he would've slapped her across the face. Grace was about to yell something when she heard another voice yell, "Stop it, both of you!"

Raelynn was standing on the porch, watching the two of them and couldn't take it. They were being cruel to one another and there was no need for it.

She woke up and felt "funny." Looking out front, she saw that Grace was there by her car and was going to ask for her to come in and wait with her until Seth got back. After walking out on the porch, she could hear them arguing. The words were awful and she wouldn't stand for it.

Pushing Tavin aside, Grace ran around the car and up onto the porch.

"I'm sorry you heard us arguing," She said to Raelynn.

Tavin walked over and came up the steps slowly.

"Don't push each other away," Raelynn yelled at them both, "it only makes it more difficult."

Grace wasn't sure what Raelynn was talking about.

Wanting to explain, Raelynn turned around to go back inside when a pain tore through her belly. "Uhhhh," She yelled and fell to the floor.

Jumping forward, Grace saw that Raelynn was falling but didn't get to her quick enough to stop her form hitting the floor. She could see the look of agony in Raelynn's eyes and was scared.

"What is it?" Tavin asked as he knelt down beside them in the doorway.

Raelynn squeezed her eyes shut, trying to get through the excruciating pain tearing through her stomach.

She squeaked out, "I don't know."

Tavin was about to move Raelynn when he saw the blood on the floor from between her legs. His face must've said something because, when he looked up, he saw Grace looking at him and then down to the floor.

"Dear God," Grace whispered.

Without speaking, Grace took one side of Raelynn and Tavin took the other. They half lifted her from the floor up into the closest chair.

Grace's face paled when she saw the trail of blood from where they moved Raelynn. When she looked up, she could see the color leaving Raelynn's face and looked over at Tavin.

Without thinking, Grace went into auto pilot, "Tavin, call 911, I'm going to get some towels," she said calmly.

A minute later, she was back in the room, grabbing towels from the guest bathroom, and listening to Tavin talk to the 911 operator.

Raelynn was delirious now, Grace assumed from blood loss. It was coming out of her fast and Grace pushed towels up toward her pelvis to try to get the bleeding to stop.

Grace was trying to stave off full-blown panic and handed Tavin her cell phone.

"I need you to call Rich or John, whoever you can, so they can get Seth in here," She told him calmly.

Tavin wanted to throw up. He owned a ranch, saw animals hurt and bleeding all the time, but never saw this before. He nodded absently to Grace's directions and started dialing.

Raelynn reached up and took Grace's hand, "I know something's wrong," she said in a weak whisper, "tell Seth I love him so much," she got out then went limp in the chair.

Grace started crying, there was so much blood and Raelynn wasn't talking. She could hear the sound of Tavin's voice in the distance, as if he were miles away and just focused on keeping the towels pressed against Raelynn.

Tavin hung up with John and turned back to see Raelynn limp against the chair like a ragdoll. Grace was crying while pressing towels against her body.

He checked Raelynn's wrist to see if he could feel a pulse and he couldn't.

"Damn it!" He yelled and pulled Raelynn down onto the floor.

Grace watched Tavin as he positioned himself over Raelynn. He started chest compressions and counted out loud, "1-2-3-4."

He motioned to Grace, "You need to see if she's breathing," he said.

Leaning down over Raelynn, Grace tried to listen for a breath, she couldn't feel or hear anything so she shook her head at Tavin.

"You need to breathe for her," He said as she was pushing down on Raelynn's chest.

Nodding, Grace tilted Raelynn's head up and breathed for her when Tavin got to 15.

They were still doing CPR when Grace heard a commotion coming through the house.

"What the hell!" Seth screamed, "Raelynn!" He cried out and slid onto the floor next to his wife.

John knelt down next to Tavin and said, "I'm going to take over."

Tavin nodded and continued his current count. As soon as Grace leaned down to give Raelynn a breath, he moved over and let John start compressions.

The sirens were wailing and Grace kept saying to herself, 'Hold on Raelynn, they're coming.'

Her tears were streaming down her cheeks but she wiped them before she would breathe into Raelynn's mouth. She prayed the whole time that Raelynn and the baby would be okay.

Seth was crying and trying to take his wife into his arms. All he could see was the blood and his love, laying there so still.

The paramedics came in and quickly took over the CPR. One of them was asking questions and the other was inserting a tube into her mouth.

Within a few minutes, Raelynn was breathing with the help of a bag, and one paramedic was doing compressions.

Seth followed them out and got into the ambulance.

John wrapped his arms around Grace and steered her out the door.

"We're going to the hospital," John said calmly.

Tavin followed them out, trying to avoid passing out from exhaustion. His ribs hurt like hell from doing the compressions.

The drive to the hospital took forever even though it was only 25 minutes away.

Grace sat in the back seat, with Tavin's arm around her, and stared into nothing.

John drove as fast as he could and called Melissa.

Hearing her aunt's frantic tone, Grace started crying again.

They pulled into the hospital in Pearland and everyone got out.

The ambulance already arrived and Raelynn was already taken back to wherever they were treating her. Seth was nowhere to be found so they assumed he went back with her.

The three of them sat down in the waiting area and said nothing.

A nurse came out and, seeing Grace and Tavin with blood all over them, came running up.

Grace wanted to explain that it wasn't her blood but the words wouldn't come out. She tried to stand up but, the room started spinning and turning black.

"She's in shock," Someone yelled.

The darkness faded and Grace opened her eyes. She was in a lowly lit room, the soft light decorating the room with shadows.

Focusing, Grace's eyes moved around until they fell on a sleeping Tavin. He was sitting upright in a chair and looking very uncomfortable. She smiled despite the fact that she should be hating him completely for his words, she thought he looked wonderful.

She moved her head and felt achy. Nothing hurt really, it was more of an emotional thing.

"Hi," Melissa whispered as she walked over to the side of her niece's bed.

Grace turned to see her aunt, looking like hell, but smiling down at her.

Trying to find her voice, Grace croaked out, "Hi yourself."

Melissa took her niece's attempt at humor as a good sign.

Trying to sit up, Grace asked, "What happened?"

Tears coming to her eyes, Melissa pulled a chair over and sat down. She took her niece's hand into her own and rubbed the back of it in a soothing motion.

"Raelynn," Melissa started to say and her voice cracking as the emotion engulfed her.

Panic was starting to set into Grace's chest. 'No,' she screamed inside. Tears rand down her cheeks.

Melissa could see where Grace's thoughts were going and half smiled.

Kissing her niece's hand, she reassured her, "No baby, she's okay."

Relief poured over Grace like a summer rain onto a field of wildflowers. She soaked it up into her mind and took a deep breath.

"She had placenta previa so the place where the placenta attached was too close to her cervix. It pulled away so that's what started the bleeding," Melissa relayed the information as she heard it from the doctor.

Grace nodded and asked, "Where is she now?"

Melissa smiled, and said, "She's in ICU, she had to have a blood transfusion and they're making sure she stays stable."

Crying again, Grace choked out, "And the baby?"

"Oh," Melissa said happily, "a little girl," she pulled out her phone, "she's a little small but holding her own."

Grace smiled, "Oh my goodness," she sighed as she looked at the 2 pictures Melissa was able to snap of the little baby.

Wiping a tear from her face, Melissa sat up and said, "You know, you and Tavin saved her life."

Looking up from the phone, Grace felt humbled, "No," she answered.

Nodding Melissa repeated, "You saved her life," she sniffled, "and I will be forever thankful to you for it."

Smiling through her tears, Grace looked over to see that Tavin was gone from the chair he'd been sleeping in.

Chapter 26

Tavin was walking down the hall in a haze. He woke up to hear Grace and Melissa talking. Once he was sure Grace was okay, he quietly left the room. He knew his presence would upset her.

The things he said to her at the ranch were hurtful. He was hurt by what she said too and knew he had to reconcile that.

"Hey," Seth said as he came out of the restroom.

He'd needed a moment to splash some water on his face and soak in all that happened tonight.

Tavin nodded in acknowledgment, "Hey yourself," he smiled and asked, "how are the ladies?"

Smiling, Seth answered, "Raelynn is doing pretty well, they'll still need to watch her for a couple of days," he ran his fingers through his already tousled hair, "Our little Hannah is doing pretty good too."

Taking in the info, Tavin whispered, "Hannah," as if testing out the name.

Placing his hand on Tavin's shoulder, Seth tried to clamp down on his emotion as he talked.

"The doctor said if you and Grace hadn't started CPR then and tried to stop the bleeding, we would've lost her," Seth said.

Tavin's heart ached, "I'm glad we were there."

Nodding, Seth stated, "Me too brother," they started walking down the hall, "I would've have been gone if I'd lost her."

Tavin just listened to his friend, never having heard Seth talk like this moved him.

"She is my whole world," Seth said, "she made me come alive."

With another pat on the shoulder, Seth smiled and walked toward the sign saying ICU.

Tavin stood in the hallway and watched him go.

Standing there, he wondered how he would feel if something, Heaven forbid, were to happen to Grace.

He would have no one to argue with, that's for sure. There would be no thoughts of her when he woke up or wondering if he should call her all during the day. No wanting to tell her about the good things or the bad things that happened. No thinking up ways to get her goat or make her smile the way that only she could.

"Holy crap," He whispered and walked over to the nearest bench.

John and Rich found him there a while later.

Rich touched his shoulder, "Hey TJ, are you feeling okay?" He asked.

Tavin looked up at the two most honorable men he knew. He respected their opinions above all else.

"I love Grace," Tavin said loudly.

Just hearing the words come out of his mouth made him feel very weird inside. It was like having the world shift under your feet and you weren't sure where to step.

John laughed, "Really?" He asked sarcastically, "I think we could've told you that ages ago."

Rich sat down next to Tavin, "We did tell him that," he said sharply.

Tavin didn't appreciate their humor at his expense but he knew he had it coming. Unfortunately, he didn't think Grace would be accepting of his realizations now. Not after all they said to one another.

Standing up, Tavin looked at both Rich and John and asked, "What if she hates me?"

John smiled, "That's the thing about lovin someone boy," he punched Tavin in the arm lightly, "It's easy to forgive em."

Somehow Tavin didn't think it would be quite that easy but he appreciated John saying it.

Melissa came down the hall and saw the three of the sorriest looking cowboys around standing there. She smiled at the thought.

"Hello," Melissa said lightly and walked over to give John a hug and kiss.

John held her tight, "Hello my sweet lady," he answered.

Tavin watched the affection between John and Melissa and wondered how they did it. You looked at them and saw all the differences.

John was a cowboy through and through, rugged and unpolished. Melissa was all business suits and expensive perfume.

And yet, looking at them, you couldn't help but think they must understand each other well to make it work.

Maybe that's what he needed to show Grace, although they were different, it could still work.

Melissa stood in the hallway and watched Tavin and Rich walk toward the elevator. She looked up at John and smiled.

"Don't worry about the boy," John said in his Texas drawl, "he's come to his senses."

Nodding, Melissa sighed, "I hope so."

The next day, they released Grace. She was upset that she even needed to stay over at the hospital but the doctor said it was just a precaution.

Once back at her aunt's place, they sat down to finish the holiday party arrangements. According to

Seth, he got express orders from Raelynn that the party would go on, even if she wasn't there to enjoy it. They needed to celebrate their daughter coming into the world. Plus, Hailey was coming home and she needed to be reassured that everyone was okay.

So, Grace and Melissa jumped into the preparations. Everyone they talked to offered to help so it made the whole thing very easy.

In the afternoon, they went up to the hospital to see Raelynn, since she was moved out of ICU, and the baby.

Grace walked in slowly, not sure what to expect. She laughed when she saw the inside of Raelynn's hospital room.

There were flowers and balloons everywhere. It looked like a flower shop was preparing for Mother's Day and a baby shower all at once.

"My Lord," Melissa said when she saw all the get well gifts.

Raelynn smiled, "I know right?" She looked over to see Grace and said sternly, "You need to get over here right now."

Without hesitation, Grace walked over and gave Raelynn a big hug. She could see that her friend was a little weak, but no worse for the wear.

"How are you?" Grace asked.

"Pooped out," Raelynn answered, "but good."

She was about to say more when the door to the room opened. A nurse walked in with a pink blanket in her arms.

Raelynn smiled and announced, "Here she is," and reached her arms out as the nurse handed her the bundle.

Melissa and Grace waited for the nurse to back up then crowded in around Raelynn.

All Grace could see was a little scrunched up face with a little hand moving out of the top of the blanket. Her breath hitched and a tear slid down her cheek.

"I know," Raelynn said, "this is who all the commotion is about."

The women laughed. It was a special moment, seeing Raelynn holding her new little girl and the sheer joy in her eyes made Grace feel very warm.

Seth came in and found them there, all hovering over his daughter. He couldn't help but laugh.

Raelynn looked up and saw her husband, "Hello there daddy," she said and waited for him to come around the bed.

"I'll take my little girl now," Seth announced.

He wasn't sure the women would give her up.

Raelynn gently handed him his daughter. He sat down on the edge of the bed and just looked into the eyes of this precious creature and wondered how he could love her so much already.

"Hello, Miss Hannah Grace," Seth whispered to his daughter.

Grace heard Seth and she stopped talking. Did she hear him right?

Raelynn cleared her throat, "I'm sorry I didn't ask you if it was alright," she looked at Grace, "but we felt like Miss Hannah needed to have the middle name of her Godmother."

Touched beyond words, Grace stood there, her hand to her chest and looked down at the baby.

"I'm honored," Grace whispered.

Seth smiled and winked at his wife. They would all be okay, he was sure of it.

After Melissa and Grace left the hospital, they drove over to Seth and Raelynn's place to pick up some things Raelynn needed at the hospital.

Since the baby was technically a preemie, but doing well, they decided they only wanted to keep her another day or two.

Melissa was driving down the driveway when she looked over to see Grace looking out the window in a trance.

"Are you okay?" Melissa asked.

Grace nodded and answered, "Yes," she smiled, "just overwhelmed."

Melissa nodded in agreement, "I hear you there young lady."

The car stopped and they got out.

Grace was going up the stairs first, "I can't believe that Christmas is only a few days away," she said.

Melissa followed her inside and responded, "I know."

They went upstairs to Raelynn and Seth's room. There were specific instructions about what to get so they made quick work of it.

Once the bag was packed, they walked downstairs.

Tossing the bag in the trunk, Melissa turned to her niece, "I'd like to see John if you're okay with that."

Smiling, Grace answered, "Of course, let's go."

They walked around the house and out toward the main barn.

There were men all over the place, carrying things in and out of the buildings. John was standing in the center of the driveway and calling out orders. He smiled when he saw Melissa and Grace coming over.

"Well, what a pretty sight for this old cowboy," He said silkily.

Melissa blushed at his compliment and said, "Well, aren't you lucky."

John kissed the top of her head when he hugged her, "Yep," he responded.

Grace laughed. They were so cute.

Turning, John winked at Grace and asked, "Are you going to ride today?"

Wanting to, but knowing she shouldn't, Grace just shook her head no.

"That's a darn shame," John said, "poor Miss Cindy's been lonely lately."

It wasn't tough to see the guilt trip forming. Grace looked at her aunt, who was smiling, and decided to appease him.

Looking toward the barn, Grace answered, "Okay, for Miss Cindy."

Smirking, John said, "Of course."

They all laughed and walked over to the horse barn.

A few minutes later, Grace was up in a saddle. She borrowed an extra pair of boots and hat and was off into the fields.

The air was crisp but not severely cold. The breeze felt good as it mussed her hair.

She was only walking, deciding to take her time and not over work Miss Cindy. Of course, it was just her not wanting to over work herself but she was pretty sure the horse wouldn't mind.

It was easy to let her mind wander when she was out here riding. The creak of the leather saddle, the sound of the horse's breathing, the sounds of the birds and cattle in the distance; it all created a cocoon of sensory delight that settled Grace's soul.

Grace walked with Cindy for a long while. It wouldn't have surprised her if John sent Charlie out to get her, but no one came.

Darkness was setting in when she finally headed back to the ranch.

About a half mile out, Grace noticed lights from the ranch. Not the regular lights, but a whole bunch of them in one place. She urged Cindy into a trot so she could figure out what they were.

As soon as she was close enough, Grace pulled Cindy up to stop and sat in the saddle, smiling like a little kid.

The guys turned one of the barns into a glittering show of light. They were everywhere along the outside of the building.

She started up again and walked the horse around to the front of the barn.

Melissa and John were standing there, staring at the building, silly smiles on their faces.

John nodded when he spotted Grace riding up.

"What do you think?" He asked, looking up at her in the saddle.

Grace looked at the building and back to them, "I think it looks like the stars have fallen down to earth."

Melissa smiled, "What a lovely description," she commented.

One of the hands came up to her and offered to take Miss Cindy.

Grace jumped down and gave the horse a quick scratch behind the ears before she was led away. Joining John and Melissa she stood there, in awe, and smiling for absolutely no reason.

Chapter 27

The day of the Christmas party, Grace woke up early. She and Melissa were going over to the ranch to supervise the last minute preparations so Raelynn could rest and enjoy the baby.

They came home three days earlier and were greeted by an emotional Hailey.

Grace remembered how hard Raelynn held her daughters, how they cried, how Hailey looked at her little sister with love and adoration. It was such a Blessing to be around that much love.

It did no good to wish for that for herself, and yet, that's what Grace was doing. She hoped that she would find that kind of love and understanding.

Knowing that it was possible with Tavin, but he decided to push her away, only made the hurt worse.

She wanted to stay here but she wasn't sure she would be able to.

Pushing her maudlin thoughts aside, she got dressed and was determined to be festive and thankful at the party.

She came downstairs and laughed when she saw her aunt.

Melissa stood in the kitchen, hunched over the coffee maker as if it were a God, and wore the most ridiculous reindeer ears on a headband.

"Really?" Grace asked while laughing.

Melissa frowned and mumbled, "I'm trying to be in a holiday mood but the coffee won't come out fast enough.

Her aunt was just too much.

"Why don't we go out to breakfast this morning?" Grace suggested.

Tilting her head, as if she were considering the options, Melissa nodded, "Okay, anything that means I can eat soon and not cook or clean."

Grace grabbed her purse, "Okay then, let's go." She said.

The twosome ate breakfast then went out to the ranch.

As soon as they pulled up, they were greeted with a frazzled looking John.

"She's doing too much and driving us crazy," John said desperately while pointing to the house.

Melissa laughed and leaned up to kiss him soundly on the mouth.

Leaning back, Melissa asked him, "Did that help?"

John nodded but pointed to the house again, "You have to help us."

Grace tried so hard not to laugh at the tough and rumble cowboy who was reduced to ashes by one woman.

They walked up the steps and heard the noise from inside.

"Oh boy," Melissa whispered to Grace before she opened the door.

The house, was chaos. Seth, Hailey, and some of the guys were all going back and forth through the rooms and Raelynn was yelling.

Grace was about to ask her aunt what to do when she heard a blood curling whistle.

Everyone stopped and stared.

Melissa stepped forward and announced, "Now hear this, I am relieving Mrs. Rhodes from her supervisory duties. All of you will follow me outside so we don't scare the baby any more than we've already done."

Raelynn was about to say something but, one look from Melissa silenced her.

Grace had a new found respect for her aunt.

She watched everyone file out through the kitchen behind Melissa and she went over to where Raelynn was sitting......pouting.

"Oh, it's not so bad," Grace said soothingly. "At least now you can't be blamed if something goes wrong."

Raelynn raised her eyebrows and smiled, "You may have a point there," she said to Grace.

They sat and talked about the baby, Hailey, the party, and Grace was relieved that Raelynn was resting for the most part.

"I never said thank you," Raelynn said softly.

It was still an emotional thing, thinking about the fact that she almost died, and that they almost lost Hannah too.

Grace smiled, "No thanks necessary," she started, "Tavin acted first, he noticed your breathing and pulse had slowed and started CPR."

"Oh so he's the one who made my chest feel like some buffalo did a dance on it," Grace said lightly.

Nodding, Grace was happy to place the blame for that elsewhere.

Raelynn picked up her glass of lemonade and took a sip. Once she put the glass back down she looked at Grace.

"Have you seen him?" Raelynn asked.

Grace shook her head no, "I don't expect to, we were awful to one another."

Raelynn looked thoughtful, "You know, the nice thing about loving someone is that you can forgive them."

Grace would love to believe that, but she was sure Tavin was not one to say it or do it.

They moved on to other subjects but, for some reason, Grace couldn't stop hoping that she and Tavin could apologize and forgive one another.

Several hours later, guests started arriving for the party.

Everyone was out in the barn and it was lit up like a Christmas tree. There were little white lights everywhere. In the center of the room was a Christmas tree that seemed to be about 20 feet high, decorated with large ornaments in festive colors of red, gold, silver, and white.

Grace stood next to the tree as the guests came in. It was a pretty central location where she could people watch and still be available if Seth or Raelynn or Melissa needed her.

She watched Hailey dance around the floor with one of the hands and laughed at the antics of the partygoers.

The music was loud and, appropriately, county western Christmas themed.

She knew as soon as Tavin came into the building. The awareness she felt was palpable, her breathing was ragged and her pulse was unsteady. It was other-worldly since she couldn't see him.

Charlie came up beside her and smiled as he handed her a glass of punch.

"I thought you could use something," Charlie said.

He came tonight, partially because he knew Grace would be attending. She was beautiful in her dark green dress. Her hair was up in one of those complicated women hairdos and she smelled like a field of wildflowers.

Grace smiled her thanks and sipped her punch.

Tavin walked into the party and his eyes found Grace right away.

She was beautiful, all prettied up for the occasion. He wanted to go over and ask her to dance but then he saw one of the hands named Charlie walk over to her.

"Damn," He said under his breath.

Melissa nudged John's side and nodded toward her niece in one direction and Tavin in the other.

"I know that good looks and luck are wasted on the young people," John said sarcastically.

Melissa smiled, "I don't know," she said, "I think you're pretty good looking and Lord knows you're lucky to have me."

John nodded and leaned down to kiss her, "You are right about that," he answered.

Charlie excused himself and Grace was relieved. Not that he wasn't a great companion, but Grace wanted to look for Tavin and wouldn't be that rude while standing next to a friend.

She didn't have to look very far because as soon as she scanned the room, her eyes ran into Tavin's.

He stood there and looked at her, as she stood there and looked at him.

The song changed and dancers were coming on and off the floor that separated them. Grace stared at Tavin as he started to make his way toward her.

Tavin couldn't stay away from Grace any longer so he started to move toward her. She looked leery of him and he knew why.

Up to now, he'd been an ass in the first degree and didn't deserve another chance from her. But that wouldn't stop him from asking for one.

He stopped a foot away from her and smiled.

"Grace," He started, "you look lovely."

Grace blushed with his compliment.

"You do too," She answered.

He reached out and took her hand into his and held it between them.

Tavin cleared his throat, "You see, I've been an ass lately."

Grace chuckled and nodded. There was no need to confirm the obvious.

"Well," Tavin started, "I was thinking how nice it was to have someone who was willing to point that fact out to me."

His words were not making a lot of sense to Grace. She frowned, hoping he would get to the point.

Tavin snagged her free hand with his and said, "You see you saved me," he smiled, "even when I had no clue that I needed to be saved."

Grace was shocked by his words. She didn't know how to respond so she just stood there.

"I know I'm stubborn and hard to understand," He looked around then back to Grace, "but you get me."

Grace nodded in understanding and waited for him to continue.

Tavin sighed and spoke calmly, "I guess I just need you. It doesn't matter if we're fighting or loving, just as long as we're together."

It was like a dream, he was saying the words she desperately wanted to hear. But he said wonderful things to her before and then turned around and hurt her, so now she was afraid.

Tavin could see she wasn't entirely convinced yet, so he got down on one knee and looked up into her eyes. They reflected all the sparkly lights that twinkled throughout the room. It was how his heart felt every time he was with her, like little explosions of love going off.

"Grace," Tavin said as he looked up, "I'm certainly not the easiest man to love, and I'm certainly not worthy of you, but I'll work every day to prove to you that I'm the right man to make you happy."

Tears slipped down Grace's cheek. She didn't know what to say now. Looking up, she made eye contact with John. He smiled at her and nodded, as if telling her it would all be alright.

She looked down into Tavin's eyes and said, "You're right, you're not the easiest man to love," she took a breath, "you're stubborn and pigheaded and you make me want to yell and scream a lot."

He smiled up at her, knowing she spoke the truth.

"But," Grace started, "you're also the most loving man I know."

Tavin wanted to ask her to marry him, but she interrupted him.

"But just so you know," Grace said smartly, "If you don't do what you say you'll do…..love me so much I won't know what to do, I'll kick your butt."

Smiling, Tavin knew she meant every word. So did he.

Reaching into his pocket, Tavin pulled out a little black case. He chuckled at the shocked look on Grace's face. After opening the box, he lifted it up to her.

"I will give you this ring and I'll do everything in my power to make sure you're happy every single day," He said with tears filling his own eyes.

Grace couldn't speak, she just nodded to him and he slipped the ring on her finger.

When Tavin stood up, he took her in his arms and kissed her, his feelings of love poured into the kiss and enveloped them both in their own circle of love.

Applause erupted and, when they pulled apart, they noticed everyone at the party was watching them.

Grace realized, as people were coming up and congratulating them, that their love story wasn't necessarily the one made up of wine and roses, but it was theirs. And, it was real.

Melissa and John were the last ones to come up and congratulate the couple.

John clapped Tavin on the back and said, "You did pretty good there boy."

Tavin looked over and smiled, "I did okay."

Melissa hugged Grace and whispered in her ear, "I'm so happy for you. Love each other and the rest will work itself out."

"You've set such a good example," Grace whispered back, "that I'll have no choice but to be happy."

Melissa stepped away from her niece and gave Tavin a hug.

"Well, this sure does upset me some," John said from behind her.

Grace, Tavin, and Melissa all looked at him with shocked expressions on their faces.

John cleared his throat and said, "You see, I was going to bend down on one knee by this tree here and ask Melissa if she'd like me to make an honest woman of her but you two went and blew that plan up."

Her eyes wide with shock, Melissa wasn't sure she heard him right.

"I got this here ring, that Seth helped me pick out, I'm sure with Raelynn's help," He choked out as he pulled the ring out of his pocket.

Grace held Tavin's hand tight, waiting for her aunt to say something. She was floored that he proposed, as was everyone else in the room because they stopped once again.

"Uh," Melissa whispered, "yes."

That was all it took for John, he swept Melissa up into his arms and swung her around.

Raelynn and Seth were standing a few feet away and smiling at their friends.

Seth smiled at his wife and spoke first, "I guess this will be a very Merry Christmas indeed."

Nodding, Raelynn answered, "I guess so. We have family and love, what else do we need?"